MW01248827

Repo Madness: A Simpleton's Guide to the Street's Wicked Ways

by

M.E. Tuthill

ISBN 978-1-312-76555-9

©2023

"The real polarization is economic-financial: there are two economies in America and there's very little commonality in the two economies. One benefited greatly from financialization and globalization, and the other was hollowed out and brought to its knees by financialization and globalization."

---Tyler Durden

"Finance is bullshit. Math is truth."

---Harry Markopolos

"The FHLB system...may not be able to fill its roles, both as liquidity back-stop and as an integral provider of funding in credit markets, in the next financial crisis."

---*Fed Notes* October 2017

"What is this book about?
It is about the taking of collateral, *all* of it

--David Rogers Webb

Discordant music and a man writhing onstage.

--- The GFC as portray in "The Lehman Trilogy"

Let me be clear. I am the simpleton, not you. I would never call you a simpleton. I say this about myself because I am a writer, not an economist, financial analyst, or market guru.

One thing I am confident about is the fact that our monetary system is insane.

I said as much to a prominent economist in an email, and he did not refute it. Never mind the fact that he didn't reply. He did not refute my statement!

So, bear in mind that I stumbled on all this beginning in 2006 as a failed stockbroker who became a financial writer. And if by chance something is confusing, I implore you to stay with me because if you do you will come away with a sense of how crazy everything is and that is what I hope to accomplish. I want people to know it's all nuts.

M.E. Tuthill

CHAPTERS

Part I   Above Our Heads

Part II What About Us?

Part I

"Above Our Heads"

Introduction

It was March 2007 when working as a financial writer, I had an inkling something may be amiss. It was fleeting, a momentary wave of discomfort. I interviewed someone at Fitch Ratings about a new product. It was a computer program, and I began my article singing its praises, saying, "It brings to mind those cool colorful computer models you can rotate on the screen, viewing the structure from every imaginable angle." I also quoted from the Fitch pitch, "...over time the landscape and complexity of conduit portfolios has changed significantly." [1]

Well, you could say that again! This product analyzed Asset-Backed Commercial Paper. According to my interviewee, the market was booming. Approximately $1.4 trillion invested in it. Why? Because unlike the once dominant corporate commercial paper, ABCP's growth "in part was due to the fact that many low and non-investment grade rated corporations can obtain cheaper financing by issuing ABCP." He went on to explain that "These programs are collateralized by many different types of investments pooled into one product. According to Fitch (We'll call him "Fitch"), banks had agreed to absorb a percentage of the potential loss in the ABCP conduit. This percentage was called "program wide credit enhancement." Fitch said arriving at the PWCE was an "inexact science." This new product could analyze the portfolio and determine what percentage a bank would commit to backing based on the composition of the portfolio.

Fitch's website put it this way, the product, which for our purposes, will go unnamed, provides "an advanced and granular measurement of portfolio credit risk, which incorporates the credit of the underlying pool of assets, asset correlation, concentrations of a given multi-seller conduit and other credit factors." My interviewee called it a valuable "tool" providing a "more precise, quantitative approach for Fitch to evaluate programs on a regular basis."[1]

Enthusiastically I wound up the story with the following, "Let the analytics begin!" Then I got to thinking, "Shouldn't they already know what's in these products?"

It was just another day at the office, yet the question raised would obviously come back to me when the entire financial system melted down. The Federal Reserve paper, "The Evolution of the Financial Crisis: Panic in the Asset Backed Commercial Paper Market" [2] was written in 2009 by Daniel L. Covitz, Nellie Liang and Gustavo A. Suarez. In the Abstract they make the following observation, "We find evidence of extensive runs: more than 100 programs (one-third of all ABCP programs) were in a run within weeks of the onset of the turmoil and the odds of subsequently leaving the run state were very low."

On October 2014 William C. Dudley, President of the Federal Reserve Bank of New York, presented remarks to the Salomon Center for the Study of Financial Institutions in New York City.[3]

Reflecting on lessons learned from the financial crisis he observed that over time "bank funding began to shift away from unsecured funding to secured funding markets." In other words, participants "preferred holding specific collateral against their long, even short-term loans, than just *trusting* in the ongoing viability of the borrower." (My italics)

He went on to say this shift had "substantive implications" as it removed the adherence to what was believed to be the "regular activity in the unsecured (non-collateralized) interbank funding markets." As a result, those markets "dried up" to the point that "in some instance there would be no transactions for longer dated tenors."

When did this shift occur?

According to a recent paper by Lev Menand and Joshua Younger, the shift began in the 1950s under the stewardship of the Fed. The paper, "Money & the Public Debt: Treasury Market Liquidity as a Legal Phenomenon," explains how the Fed at that time, "...sought to establish a 'free market' in government debt, in large part to counter inflationary pressures." Further along they write, this shift of "central bank exiting and private actors stepping in...Required creative lawyering and ongoing government support. The lynchpin was a form of near money-money financing for non-bank dealer firms that the Fed itself developed: a sale-and-repurchase agreement." [4]

Put another way, the authors state, "As William McChesney Martin, then-Chairman of the Board of Governors of the Federal Reserve System, later put it, the capital markets (and not the banking system) 'represent the main channel through which, the Government's financial policies to foster growth and stability must pass.'"[5]

It was the inception of what would morph into a financial labyrinth that is so large, so interconnected as to defy efforts to rein it in. A system so completely out of our control that I would wager even those who profit by its ethos often would be hard pressed to explain it.

And don't take just my word for it. On September 23, 2021, President Joseph Biden nominated Professor Saule Omarova of Cornell University to head the office of Comptroller of the Currency.

On Sept. 27 the law firm of Gibson Dunn & Crutcher put out a release titled, "The U.S. Comptroller of the Currency Nominee and Her Writings: What They Mean for Banks and Fintech." [6]

Among other quotes from Omarova I have included the following, "today's financial system is growing increasingly complex and difficult to manage. This overarching trend manifests itself not only in the dazzling organizational complexity of large financial conglomerates, but also in the exponential growth of complex financial instruments – derivatives, asset-backed securities, and other structured products – and correspondingly complex markets in which they trade. The result is that it is extremely difficult to measure and analyze not only the overall pattern of risk distribution in the financial system but also the true level of individual financial firms' risk exposure."

As far back as 1987 economists and others were grappling with the very same issues that dog us today.

In August of that year a symposium was held in Jackson Hole, Wyoming. It was sponsored by the Federal Reserve Bank of Kansas City and titled, "Restructuring the Financial System."

Among the participants was Franklin R. Edwards. Edwards is a widely respected economist who is affiliated with Columbia University Graduate School of Business. His presentation asked the question, "Can Regulatory Reform Prevent the Impending Disaster in Financial Markets?"[7]

During his talk, he stated the following, "The idea that this system may in some way be seriously flawed is an alien thought. The notion that it should be drastically changed shocks us. 'If it works, don't change it' is a philosophy that needs no proselytizing. But the world is changing, and our financial system is no longer working well. Worse, it is failing in ways that are not immediately obvious, giving us a false sense of comfort. The seeds of change, planted in the 1960s, have long ago sent their shoots and to every corner of the financial landscape. Institutions are being entangled and will eventually be smothered unless the financial system is restructured to accommodate these changes."

The term "shadow banking" is credited to economist and PIMCO executive Peter McCulley who used it in his August 2007 presentation at the Fed's annual Jackson Hole, Wyoming symposium.

If one were to visualize the shadow banking system, I would say picture the entire earth encased in a web of fiber optic cables so that a view from the moon would be the earth resembling a giant ball of twine. In the confines of this giant web is the flow of money be it hedged, collateralized, or made up of other myriad configurations created by the clever machinations of those behind the curtain called Wall Street. No one has a handle on this different kind of worldwide web. Efforts are made to tame it, track it, control it all to no avail. And while I do not delude myself that I, as a single observer, can deconstruct the shadow banking system, I do hope my efforts will give you a taste of what is happening above your head.

Ellen Brown in her book, "Banking on the People, Democratizing MONEY in the DIGITAL AGE,"[8] defines shadow banking as follows, "financial intermediaries not subject to regulatory oversight involved in facilitating the creation of credit across the global financial system. It also refers to unregulated activities by regulated institutions."[8]

Insight into the shadow banking system is provided by Mary Fricker. A financial reporter who co-authored the 1989 book, "Inside Job: The Looting of America's Savings and Loans," Fricker expressed remorse over not seeing the signs that led to the crisis. Like most of us, she learned of it from media reports about the $700 billion bailout authorized by the Congress in 2008. From that moment on she has devoted herself to understanding every aspect of the shadow banking system all the while exhorting reporters to take up the cause.

Her award-winning website *RepoWatch.org* is a treasure trove of information not only about the repurchase agreement (will get to that later) but the entire shadow banking system.

Speaking to journalists in 2012 Fricker began with this statement, "Shadow banking was the epicenter of the financial crisis. Almost no reporters understood it then and not many understand it now. But it is important because it probably provides half the credit in this country, we've seen how dangerous it can be, so we need to know how to cover it going forward." [9]

Turns out Fricker wasn't the only person taken by surprise. This is what Janet Yellen said to the Financial Crisis Inquiry Commission in 2010, "For my own part, I did not see and did not appreciate what the risks were with the securitization, the credit ratings agencies, the shadow banking system, the SIVs—I didn't see any of that coming until it happened." [10] As you will see later, the New York Fed also came late to the party. That's not to say there weren't those who raised concerns. The only problem was the concerns were met with deaf ears.

In his 2012 paper, "Restructuring the Banking System to Improve Safety and Soundness,"[11] Thomas M. Hoenig, at the time Vice Chairman of the Federal Deposit Insurance Corporation along with Kansas City Fed vice-president, Charles S. Morris, explained the change, "Whereas the traditional banking model of making loans and holding them to maturity earned profits from the loan-deposit rate spreads, the shadow banking model earns profits from fees and transactions."

Hoenig's comments were echoed by New York Fed president Dudley during a February

2013 speech before the New York Bankers Association titled, "Fixing Wholesale Funding to Build a More Stable Financial System." Dudley told them, "As this audience knows, In the two decades before the financial crisis, the global financial system underwent rapid transformation. During this period, there was a shift from bank-based financial intermediation to capital markets based financial intermediation, and an increase in the scale and complexity of securitization activities." (Securitization occurs when multiple investment instruments, say loans for example, are pooled together, packaged, and transacted as one security.)[12]

This is just a fancy way of saying that during the decades leading up to the crisis the Wizards of Wall Street hijacked the country's financial markets with sophisticated, complicated investment activities with the sole purpose of generating the most wealth for those with access to those superfast conduits above our heads. If the shadow banking system were to make a sound it would be the whizzing of trillions of transactions taking place in nanoseconds powered by algorithms created by the "best and brightest" on the Street.

This strikes a chord with me. It is sad that we have come to this. One can safely say that to yearn for a simpler time is not in this case, built on the illusion that "back in the day" our lives were better, simpler, more honest. In this case it is true.

It all began to change in the 1950s when an agreement was reached between the Treasury and Fed solidifying the Fed's power as the country's central bank. It was this agreement that gave the Fed full control over monetary policy, and it wasn't long after that ever so stealthily the seeds of the Global Financial Crisis would begin to take hold.

And the sad fact is the banks failed to uphold their end of the bargain. At that 1987 symposium E. Gerald Corrigan, then New York Federal Reserve President put it this way, "There is a lot of talk about the safety net and particularly on two important elements of the safety net: deposit insurance-whatever one may think of it-and the discount window. But there is some tendency to forget that the process of supervision and regulation itself constitutes the third leg of the safety net. It's not the payments system. Access to the payments system is part of the quid pro quo that goes with being subject to supervision. But I do not regard the payments system in and of itself or access to it-as part of the safety net, but a privilege extended to banks as part of their public role and as part of the quid pro quo" [13].

As quoted in the Gibson Dunn release Comptroller of the Currency nominee Professor Omarova alluded to what Corrigan had said so many years ago, stating that Corrigan had "argued that, in exchange for the publicly-conferred benefits uniquely available to them, banks have an obligation to align their implicit codes – and their actual conduct – with the public good. In practice, however, there has been little evidence of such an alignment. One of the most troubling revelations about bank conduct before the Financial Crisis was that, in the vast majority of these cases, banks and their employees' socially harmful and ethically questionable business conduct was perfectly permissible under the existing legal rules. In each of those instances, bankers voluntarily, and often knowingly, chose to pursue a particular privately lucrative but socially suboptimal business" [14]

A predominant feature of the shadow banking system is what is called "wholesale funding." Wholesale funding was a term that mystified me. What did it entail? What exactly was it?

Today, I searched out a definition and here is what I came up with from Investopedia, "Wholesale money refers to the large sums of money lent by financial institutions in the money markets. This wholesale banking encompasses the market for tradable securities, such as Treasury bills, commercial paper, bankers' acceptances, foreign or brokered deposits, certificates of deposit, bills of exchange, repo agreements, federal funds, and short-lived mortgage and asset-backed securities." It is further stated that "Wholesale funding sources include, but are not limited to, Federal funds, public funds (such as state and local municipalities), U.S. Federal Home Loan Bank advances, the U.S. Federal Reserve's primary credit program, foreign deposits, brokered deposits, and deposits obtained through the Internet or CD listing services ..." [15]

Note the phrase, "not limited to." Fricker's 2012 presentation includes a long list of shadow banking participants among them are traditional banks, insurance companies among other corporations, mutual funds, pensions, endowments, housing behemoths, Fannie and Freddie Mac and the

Federal Home Loan banks.[16] And this is just a partial list! In other words, the wholesale funding markets are gargantuan. And as if we need another differentiator, it is interesting to note that Yale professor and shadow banking expert, Gary Gorton said the crisis of '08 was a "wholesale" panic unlike earlier crises which he described as "retail" panics. In other words, we weren't in Kansas anymore.[17]

In Dudley's previously mentioned paper on wholesale funding, he states that "The growing reliance on short-term wholesale funding to finance longer-term assets increased liquidity and maturity mismatch risk."

Dudley went on to say, "Short-term funding of longer-term assets is inherently unstable." He then called for "curtailing short-term wholesale finance in the system." [18]

And dare I say he lives in an alternative universe. This was prompted by his call for "prudent regulation." It has become clear to me that regulators are woefully ill-equipped to keep pace with financial innovations being conjured up by Wall Street. Maybe Superman could keep up with a speeding train, but not regulators. It is all moving too fast.

What he says next beggars the imagination. He suggests that one could look to expansion of the "range of financial intermediation activity that is directly backstopped by the central bank's lender of last resort function."

It is remarkable that he would say this post the Global Financial Crisis. At the same time, he was prescient for the Fed has become the lender of last resort as evidenced by its massive and unprecedented Covid-19 bailout.

At one point he even goes as far as to liken the "lender of last resort" (the Fed) to the FDIC which may one day look toward to Fed for similar relief. Print baby print!!

And finally, there's Zoltan Pozsar. Or as efinancialcareers.com's Sarah Butcher wrote in July 2021, the "oracle of market plumbing."[19]

In her article she recounts Pozsar's path which eventually landed him at Credit Suisse as managing director of short-term interest rate strategy.

Born in Rumania, he took an unconventional path. Eschewing Wharton and Harvard, he earned his MBA in Korea.

Following were stints at Moody's Investor Services, the New York Fed, the International Monetary Fund, and the Department of the Treasury, and then Credit Suisse in 2015.

In 2010 while at the New York Fed, Pozsar co-wrote a paper with Tobias Adrian, Adam Ashcraft and Hayley Boesky. Titled, "Shadow Banking." Its abstract described the prominent players in the shadow banking system. "Shadow banks are financial intermediaries that conduct maturity, credit, and liquidity transformation without explicit access to central bank liquidity or public sector credit guarantees." [20]

While researching this book I have read many books and have unabashedly referenced them throughout. Pozsar's name came up in Danielle DiMartino Booth's book, "Fed Up."[21] Thinking I had "seen it all" I soon realized I hadn't when I read the following quote attributed to Pozsar, "There was no institutionalized effort to understand the shadow banking system until I got to the Fed." According to Booth, Pozsar arrived at the New York Fed in August of 2008.

I recall pulling up Pozsar's 2010 paper on my computer. The map of the shadow banking system on page 10 stopped me in my tracks. It was all too much. The complexity was overwhelming to a neophyte (or anyone else). So instead of studying it I printed it out and took it to Staples. I decided to take the image and turn it into shadow banking placemats.

Now to the book. Mary Fricker explains that repurchase agreements and securities lending are integral to shadow banking. Without securities and these constructs shadow banking would not exist. Part I of the book addresses repurchase agreements, the larger of the two markets. In addition, it takes a trip down memory lane by examining two incidents in the 1980s that informed its creation. Next up is collateral. Every one of these deals has collateral. The role it plays is too big to ignore and finally the section concludes with a look at securities lending and a paper by the New York Fed.

In Part II the book pivots. Instead of mechanics, this section provides first-hand accounts by prominent economists and others that give the lie once and for all that there is any social benefit from this economic system. Furthermore, it lays bare the arrogance and myopic vision displayed by those placed in positions of power leading up to the crisis. Trust me, it is worth slogging through the first half to get to the second.

At the end of the book, I reveal my final assessment of the situation. I say final because it follows two, previous "so-called" solutions which I subsequently learned are not doable. It is sadly, a very pessimistic view of what comes next. I borrow liberally from David Rogers Webb's 2023 book, "The Great Taking." It is an indictment of the system based on regulatory obfuscation and legal maneuvers whose total aim is to confiscate our property rights during the next crisis. Sheer luck sent it to me, and I feel fortunate to be able to share it with you.

Chapter One

REPO

"In fact, the repo market was ground zero for the financial crisis and remains a key source of `funding for a wide variety of assets..."

---Tracy Alloway

It wasn't that many years ago when searching for "repo" on the internet resulted in a series of sites about car repossession.

The financial crisis changed that and now when searching you will come up with "repurchase agreement" or "repo."

Often referred to as "arcane" or "a dark corner" of the markets it is time to shed light on it. After all, according to the Finadium website, as of June 2021 the global repo market is estimated at $13.2 trillion![1]

Launched in 2005, Finadium describes itself as "an independent consultancy in capital markets, with a unique expertise in securities finance, collateral, and derivatives."

Repo is part of the wholesale funding market, also referred to as the "secondary market." That is the market that trades in cash or securities already owned. In a repurchase agreement the lender provides cash to the borrower for a short term, often overnight. In exchange for the cash the borrower provides securities (collateral) with the promise to buy them back or repurchase them later at a slightly higher price thus closing out the deal.

"What is the repo market? And why does it matter?" was published on the Brookings Institute's website on January 28, 2020. Authored by Jeffrey Cheng and David Wessel, it explains why repo matters. [2]

"The repo market allows financial institutions that own lots of securities (e.g., banks, broker-dealers, hedge funds) to borrow cheaply and allows parties with lots of spare cash (e.g., money market mutual funds) to earn a small return on that cash without much risk, because securities, often U.S. Treasury securities, serve as collateral."

According to a 2013 paper published by the Federal Reserve Bank of New York,[3] repo transactions consist of "six key variables: the size of the transaction, the interest rate, the type of eligible collateral, the haircut, the maturity date, and the counterparties."

The size of the transaction is self-explanatory, the interest rate is the amount the borrower pays the lender when the cash is returned to the lender. According to the website Trading Economics the "Overnight repo rate is the interest rate at which different market participants swap treasuries for cash to cover short-term cash needs. The repo rate helps to ensure banks have the liquidity to meet their daily operational needs and maintain sufficient reserves. The repo rate usually trades in line with the Federal Reserve's target interest rate."[4] As of November 12, 2021, the rate was 0.06 percent.

Next up is the collateral. That is in the case of repo the securities held by the lender. And while technically speaking participants in the transaction are called counterparties, in the vernacular used the term "counterparty" almost always refers to the party providing collateral.

A haircut is a percentage shaved off the loan amount as protection against a potential drop in the collateral. The paper provides an example. Say $100 in securities collateralizes a $98 loan then the haircut would be two percent. According to the FRBNY "The level of haircut will typically reflect the quality of collateral but may also vary by counterparty reflecting collateral provider credit worthiness." The riskier the collateral the larger the haircut. And in times of stress, it can be quite large.

The maturity date is the tenor of the transaction. Most repo transactions are short-term; overnight.

To add context here is an excerpt from a 2010 article published by *Mother Jones*.[5] And while the author, Kevin Drum, is a self-proclaimed layman, I think he explains it rather well. "To make a long story short, the repo market is basically a market for short-term loans. Really short term: it's an overnight market, and if you have, say, $100 million in repo funding you have to roll over that funding every single day. If you can't, you're in big trouble.

"To a layman that sounds crazy. Investment banks weren't just using the repo market to gain a bit of additional flexibility, they were using it as a significant part of their funding base. They were literally dependent for their continued existence on a line of funding that had to be renewed daily."

Then, there is the reverse repo. With the reverse repo it is the lender who takes the cash as collateral and provides the securities to the borrower and again, agrees to buy them back at a slightly higher price. And just like the above example when the securities are returned the borrower pays interest to the lender at the going rate.

In September of 2021, *Bankrate*'s Sara Foster posed a question in her article about repo titled, "The repo market, explained — and why the Fed has pumped hundreds of billions into it."[6] She asked why repo? And answered, "Because it ultimately benefits them. Financial firms with large pools of cash would prefer to not just let that money sit around — it doesn't collect interest, meaning it doesn't make any money."[6]

Meanwhile in an April 4, 2014, piece published in *The New York Times* titled "Time to Reduce Repo Risk,"[7] expert, Jennifer Taub wrote the following, "Most are aware that banks take in deposits from the public and then loan them out to others. They also do more: They borrow money from cash-rich investors which they use to invest in securities. The cash lenders want some collateral. But they also want the ability to give back the collateral to the bank and get their cash. That's the repo agreement. The repo market remains obscure even though it has been written about (for glazed-over eyes) for years and the collapses of Bear Stearns and Lehman in 2008 were caused when repo lenders pulled their funding."

She likens the repo to a car loan. "An overnight repo would be like you having a car loan that is due in full every morning and if the lender does not renew your loan that day, you need to find a new one, each and every day or they take your car away."

It is inconceivable that to this day the average person doesn't know about this market that informs practically every institution dealing with financial matters. Domestic and foreign banks, corporations, pensions, mutual funds, insurance companies, the U.S. Treasury, the Fed, states, and municipalities all are participants in this market. A market I have been researching for years foraging through papers, articles, books all about repo. And just once did I come across a politician saying the words, "repurchase agreement."

Plucked from the list of market participants are 25 financial institutions designated as primary dealers. This includes such luminaries as Goldman Sachs and Deutsche Bank. Being a primary dealer affords them the ability to trade directly with the government. In turn, they are required to meet certain requirements meant to underscore their strength. This is all well and good until you read on the New York Fed site that yes, this is so, but there is no auditing to ensure it is the case.

While repo was utilized by the Fed as early as 1918 it was not predominant until many decades later. It is interesting to note that repo ramped up just around the same time as the previously referred to Monetary Accord of 1951. This act addressed what was an increasing role of government in the Federal Reserve's policies during World War II.

The act, between the U.S. Secretary of the Treasury and the Fed, reestablished the Federal Reserve's independence paving the way for the Fed's control of monetary policy as the nation's central bank.

The *New York Times* reporter, Michael Quint writing on May 20, 1982, explains, "Government securities dealers invented the repurchase agreement after World War II as a substitute for a bank loan.

"These agreements, known as repos, call for the dealer to sell securities with an agreement to repurchase them at a specified price on a specified date. They have increased their use of overnight repos to a recent level of $50 billion.

"Both banks and securities dealers also offer to lend money to customers who have securities available for collateral. Called matched sale purchase transactions, or reverse repos, these deals allow a firm to earn a profit by borrowing (securities) via repos, at a lower rate than it lends, through reverse repos."[8] In fact, it was the Fed, not securities dealers, who created the present day repurchase agreement as noted in the Menand and Younger paper previously cited.

The authors point out the following, "Repo-financed liquidity lowered the cost of servicing the nation's debt and buttressed the foundations of what became known as the global dollar system." This, they write, "...had profound consequences for the U.S. economy and financial system. Deep public debt markets helped dealer firms manage their interest rate risk. That, in turn, facilitated deeper and more liquid capital markets in debt securities issued by corporations and other borrowers. The rise of dealer repo also increasingly crowded out bank deposits. In this way, the events of the 1950s and the transition to a free market in Treasuries catalyzed the growth of "shadow banking," redirecting vast supplies of corporate cash away from regulated banks."[9]

And here is the best part of all, "Ultimately, the result was a multi-trillion-dollar repo market that collapsed in 2008, bringing down many of its key players. In effect, a feature of the primary dealer system—

that repo behaved like money in many respects, but was not insured by the government or subject to bank regulation was revealed to be a *bug*." (My italics) [10]

Writing in June of 1983, Quint of *The New York Times* put it this way, "Wall Street is full of middlemen whose business is to bring buyers and sellers together and extract a profit along the way. In the Treasury market, the world's largest securities market, with more than five times the dollar volume of the New York Stock Exchange, middlemen have carved a special niche. Because there is no central trading floor for Treasury issues, a handful of little-known broker firms have evolved to execute trades between securities firms."

Writes Quint, "The Treasury brokers could be the only firms on Wall Street to rejoice over a $200 billion Federal budget deficit. *To them, large deficits mean big trading volume and big profits*, whether prices are rising or falling. Although brokers do not publicize their revenues or profits, everyone in the business is said to be making a good living." (My italics) [11]

The repo market came into its own in the 1970s and 80s. Expert Scott Skyrm explains, "By the end of the 1970s, fundamental changes in the market had begun. Growth in the Repo market followed the growth of U.S. government debt and new institutions began entering the Repo market; the size of the U.S. Repo market was at $14.8 billion in 1977."[12] Quite a jump from $14.8 billion in 1977 to $50 billion by 1982!

Just ten years earlier, money-market funds had been created to offer higher rates than traditional bank accounts.

In their previously referenced paper, "Money & the Public Debt," Menand and Younger wrote the following, "The invention of the money market mutual fund (MMF) in 1972 (when the SEC approved the listing of the Reserve Fund) was a watershed moment. These new vehicles provided individual and corporate savers with streamlined and simplified access to short-term wholesale interest rates through a closed-end mutual fund organized under the Investment Company Act of 1940. In addition to essentially eliminating the operational burden of managing these portfolios—non-trivial in an over-the-counter market with many diverse counterparties and daily rollover requirements—they also provided same-day liquidity guarantees, which imbued MMF shares with even more explicit deposit-like features."[13]

And by the 1980s with a short-term strategy, they served as a perfect vehicle for repurchase agreements. According to the website, Infoplease.com, a taxable money-market fund was returning 12.86% in 1980! Today their 7-day yield is 0.03%.[14]

What is important to emphasize here is that the repo market was/is fueled by debt. Its growth is in direct correlation with increases in the Federal deficit. Why? Because to keep it growing there must be a large store of collateral. Treasuries fit the bill. While Gordon Gekko was famous for his "Greed is good" remark in the movie, "Wall Street," when it comes to repo "debt is good."

Skrym tells us, "By the early 1980s, the Repo market was the largest single securities market in the world."[15] The largest single securities market in the world! Yet, no one really knows about it. I happened upon an economics professor who was the daughter-in-law of my neighbor. She taught at a very prestigious college. Standing outside my neighbor's house, I asked her what she thought of repo. "Repo?" she replied. Had never heard of it. And this was well after the

1980s. She did not know about a market pegged by Skrym at $200 billion in 1986.

One reason she may be out of the loop is that repo would be a challenge to teach. I am a literary person and delving into the numbers involved here has been daunting. And after years of investigation, I am of the belief that all this is misguided, misdirected, and menacing to you and me. No matter how many papers sing the praises of repo as a vital and indispensable trading model, I for one, disagree. It is, for me, madness.

The Financial Crisis Inquiry Report put it this way in 2011, "...repos have a long history, but they proliferated quickly in the 1970s. Wall Street securities dealers often sold Treasury bonds with their relatively low returns to banks and other conservative investors, while then investing the cash proceeds of these sales in securities that paid higher interest rates. The dealers agreed to repurchase the Treasuries—often within a day—at a slightly higher price than that for which they sold them (the repo rate). This repo transaction—in essence a loan—made it inexpensive and convenient for Wall Street firms to borrow.

"Because these deals were essentially collateralized loans, the securities dealers borrowed nearly the full value of the collateral, minus a small 'haircut' (to protect against a slight decline in value) ...repos were renewed, or 'rolled over,' frequently." The report went on to say that this form of borrowing could be considered, "hot money because lenders could quickly move in and out of these investments in search of the highest returns, they could be a risky source of funding."[16]

Recall what the former Kansas City Federal Reserve chief Thomas M. Hoenig, had to say about this "new," kind of banking. Remember earlier?[17] He was quoted as saying the profits were generated by transactions and fees. Wholesale funding, fee generation and lightning speed movement of money within the confines of those fiber optic cables above our heads is the order of the day. And as all this continues, we are oblivious, unschooled, and uninformed. And that's just the way they like it!

A December 2013 paper authored by Tobias Adrian, Brian Begalle, Adam Copeland and Antoine Martin of the New York Fed put it this way, "Repos are especially important for allowing arbitrage in the Treasury, agency, and agency mortgage-backed securities markets."[18] Arbitrage?

There are different types of repos among them, bilateral and tri-party. Bilateral repo is conducted between the two parties transacting the exchange. According to The Securities Industry and Financial Markets Association (SIFMA) website, "Bilateral repo is preferred when market participants want to interact directly with each other or if specific collateral is requested." Tri-party repo is conducted with an intermediary; an agent who handles the operational aspects of the trade and ensures that collateral is in place. Currently, BNY Mellon serves as the tri-party clearing house. Pre-crisis there were concerns relating to tri-party repos and how they were processed. Long story short, at one point in the day, the clearing bank was exposed to market risk. In essence it was fronting money on faith that the players would make good in short order. Reforms have since been put in place to mitigate this risk.

And says SIFMA, "There is also the general collateral finance (GCF) repo market, which is offered by the Fixed Income Clearing Corporation (FICC), a central clearing counterparty. The GCF repo is predominantly used by securities dealers, who negotiate the trade on an anonymous basis and then submit it to FICC. FICC then interposes itself as the legal counterparty to both sides of the repo transaction."[19]

Another cheerleader for repo is the International Capital Markets Association. ICMA is based in Zurich, Switzerland. What is most stunning about its mission statement is the sheer lack of cohesion it purports to accomplish. For example, its online mission statement includes the following, *"Encouraging information flows and dialogue between all participants in the international capital markets: borrowers, intermediaries and investors, and service providers, including trading platforms, clearing houses and law firms."* (my italics).[20]

That's just one of several bullet points underscoring the goal; to have a uniform, international market which is traceable at every level. It reminds me of my friend Fitch and his computer model. Let the analytics begin! Never going to happen.

For years the industry has been trying to implement what is called the Legal Entity Identifier. According to the Office of Financial Research*,[21] "The Legal Entity Identifier (LEI) is a reference code — like a bar code — used entity identifier enabling risk managers and regulators to identify parties to financial transactions instantly and precisely.

A large international bank, for example, may have an LEI identifying the parent entity plus an LEI across markets and jurisdictions to uniquely identify a legally distinct entity .   "The LEI is designed to be a linchpin for financial data — the first global and unique identifier for each of its legal entities that buy or sell stocks, bonds, swaps, or engage in other financial market transactions." Dream on.

The LEI arose from the fallout of Lehman Brothers during the crisis. One of the major exacerbators was the fact that no one could measure Lehman's exposure throughout the globe. This led to panic selling and well, we all know how that went.

Meanwhile the Bank for International Settlements has put forth criteria for "simple, transparent and comparable securitizations."

According to Wikipedia the BIS, "is an international financial institution owned by central banks that fosters international monetary and financial cooperation and serves as a bank for central banks."

*The Office of Financial Research was created as an independent entity within Dodd-Frank. Established as a department reporting to the Treasury, the Office is tasked with (1) collecting and standardizing data, (2) performing applied research and essential long-term research; and (3) developing risk measurement and monitoring tools.

On its website it explains the features of a STC. "Criteria promoting simplicity refer to the homogeneity of underlying assets with simple characteristics, and a transaction structure that is not overly complex.

"Criteria on transparency provide investors with sufficient information on the underlying assets, the structure of the transaction and the parties involved in the transaction, thereby promoting a more thorough understanding of the risks involved. The form in which the information is available should not hinder transparency, but instead it should support investors in their assessment.

"Criteria promoting comparability could assist investors in their understanding of such investments and enable more straightforward comparison between securitization products within an asset class."[22]

Hey, it's worth a shot.

How convenient that on June 21, 2021, ICMA provided a four-plus minute video on the virtues of repo. The woman with a British accent begins by saying that "Repo is one of the most vital components of the financial markets." She continues "...repo is the way that banks and other financial institutions borrow and lend cash or securities, often bonds to each other for short periods of time." She likens it to plumbing, adding just like the plumbing in our homes, we don't think about it until something goes wrong. Because this piece is pro-repo, there is no further elaboration on that point!

According to our narrator the European repo market "has an estimated turnover of €6,000,000,000,000 a day." Bear in mind those fiberoptic cables over our heads and the €6,000,000,000,000 traveling at a rapid clip spitting out miniscule profits that add up to real money. [23]

Meanwhile, a Nov. 2021 article by *Securities Finance Times* pegs the market at €8.72 trillion also as of June 2021. Which is it? Six trillion or almost nine trillion? [24]

According to our narrator, the cash from repo is used to "fund the day-to-day trading of investment banks and hedge funds."

Investment banks and hedge funds engage in sophisticated trading strategies. This raises the question, "How are those riskier entities using the cash they receive from repo?"

And ask yourself, with trillions of dollars daily changing hands among these firms and institutions how does this help the person who is beneath the world wide web of monetary manipulation? With record-low interest rates it is almost like free money for those who engage in the more advanced, innovative transactions while the rest of us wallow in a world of hideously low returns for our money.

This unidentified woman concludes that "...repo transactions happen every day on a huge scale, but with minimal risk, allowing the financial markets to run smoothly. Maintaining market liquidity, facilitating the flow of collateral, and ultimately supporting the global economy."

Today the Fed has three repo facilities. The ON RRP, which refers to the Overnight Reverse Repo Program and the recently created SRF, Standing Repo Facility and FIMA, Foreign and International Monetary Authorities Repo Facility.

The ON RRP was established in 2013. Meanwhile on July 28, 2021, the NY Fed announced the establishment of the SRF and the FIMA repo facilities stating, "These facilities will serve as backstops in money markets to support the effective implementation of monetary policy and smooth market functioning."

The market wasn't functioning so smoothly in 2019 when a dramatic spike in repo rates took everyone by surprise. Rates that generally hovered between 2 and 2.5 percent shot up to 8 or 9 percent! Christopher

Leonard in his book, "The Lords of Easy Money: How the Federal Reserve Broke the American Economy,"[25] tells of yet, another bailout stemming from this anomaly.

According to Leonard a hedge fund was investing heavily in Treasury repo, reaping profits from the sheer volume of the trades and how each was timed out. Long story short, the increase not only wiped out any returns but also squeezed margins to the extent that without relief, the fund would fail. Once again, the Fed would bailout a Wall Street entity. This time, according to Leonard, to the tune of $400 billion. All done "on the quiet."

And we would come to learn there would be more bailouts "on the quiet." And then the not so quiet bailouts like Silicon Valley Bank.

Finally, at the risk of being redundant, I want to close this chapter with a quote from Darrell Duffie. Duffie is a Distinguished Professor of Management and Finance at Stanford University's Graduate School of Business. He is ubiquitous in shadow banking circles, having written extensively about it. All the papers and lectures, however, do not alter the truth and here he speaks it. In a 2016 paper titled, "Financial Regulatory Reform After the Crisis: An Assessment," he tells us, "While progress has been made, the infrastructure of the United States securities financing markets is still not safe and sound. The biggest risk is that of a fire sale of securities in the event of the inability of a major broker dealer to roll over its securities financing under repurchase agreements."[26]

Chapter Two

THE DRYSDALE AFFAIR

"The human desire to become rich beyond all dreams of avarice will always be there. Each firm has to be guided by rules of commonsense."

--Ralph Peters
Government Securities Dealer

On June 15, 1982, Drysdale Securities Firm ceased doing business. The 92-year-old firm could lay its failure at the feet of the repo market.

"Through Abrupt Personality Change, Tiny Wall Street Firm Demonstrates the Allure, and Danger, in Speculative Trading" was published by The *Washinton Post* on May 23, 1982. Written by James L. Rowe, Jr. and Merrill Brown stated, "Until seven months ago, Drysdale Securities Corp. was a small, old-line brokerage firm that had not made many waves on Wall Street.

"Then, in an abrupt change of personality, the firm began buying huge amounts of U.S. Treasury bonds, thrusting itself into one of the biggest and most volatile of the financial markets. Some of its neighbors began to take notice.

"Late last year, the New York Stock Exchange called in officials of the 92-year-old firm to caution that heavy trading in government securities was a high-risk, big stakes business that might not be appropriate for a company of Drysdale's size. To protect brokerage customers, the Exchange tries to make sure member firms have enough assets to conduct business safely. Exchange officials suggested that Drysdale should establish a separate trading firm to deal in government securities. Drysdale did."[1]

And it would only be a few months before the Exchange's concerns were realized.

Ron Scherer's May 27,1982 piece in *The Christian Science Monitor* titled, "How Drysdale affair almost stymied US securities market" alerted the wider public to what was going on. [2] Though, in truth, the story would nary make a ripple.

It was the evening of Sunday, May 16, 1982, when a Drysdale Government Securities official called an executive of Chase Manhattan bank. The news was not good. Drysdale was short $160 million in interest payments (the figure would later be adjusted to $270 million) due on $3.2 billion in Treasuries Chase held for Drysdale as an agent servicing 30 broker/dealers. The broker/dealers traded Drysdale's Government securities to use in repo transactions. Would the bank be able to front the money?

Knowledge of the burgeoning repo market was evident in the financial reporting at the time. It appears the observers were hard pressed to put a finger on the pulse of what any sane person would say was frenetic market activity dealing in billions of dollars daily.

In any case, May 15, 1982, was the day accrued interest came due on Treasuries.

Broker/dealers representing those who temporarily owned those Treasuries as part of Drysdale's reverse repo transaction, were expecting to receive the interest they generated.

But Drysdale did not have the cash on hand to pay out and so a phone call was made.

In its role, Chase executed the trades. Actual securities never changed hands as the transactions were tracked on an in-house Chase reporting system. Drysdale's account was considered an escrow account and at the time Chase did not appreciate that it had any responsibility or connection to what transpired in it.

While Chase balked at being associated with Drysdale, it nonetheless deemed the situation too precarious to ignore. Scherer reported that according to Chase spokesman, Fraser Seitel, "Chase determined that if it did not make the payments, the entire government securities market may have come to a halt because of a breakdown in confidence." And ultimately at the urging of the Federal Reserve, Chase and another custodian, Manufacturers Hanover Trust would pay the piper. The latter bank's tally was considerably smaller than Chase's with $20 million owed.

A meeting was held at the Federal Reserve of New York between Chase and the 30 broker/dealers owed the interest. Initially Chase agreed to fork over $90 million if the b/ds would forgive the rest. No go.

As Scherer explains it, Drysdale operated largely in the secondary market. That is, as stated earlier, the market comprised of securities already owned.

According to a website, workers.org,[3] this episode began when a group of middle managers at Drysdale Securities, LLC., decided to raise $5 million to trade in the Government Securities market—a $500 billion market.[3] Within a relatively short time the group had attracted an array of customers.

Because the actual strategies employed were not disclosed to the public it was left to observers to speculate on how Drysdale made its money.

In the Scherer piece one unrelated market participant surmised that Drysdale may have been engaged in a "matchbook trading strategy," taking advantage of miniscule differences in interest rates to squeeze out modest gains or on the flipside, modest losses.

The *New York Times*, too, could not explain exactly what led to Drysdale's woes. Michael Quint reported on May 20, 1982, that while the business practices were not disclosed "it is clear that the firm was deeply immersed in the mushrooming practice of taking and extending short-term loans collateralized with Treasury securities."[4]

In that same edition, Robert J. Cole's piece "Chase Bank Will Pay Off Interest of Defaulting Bond Dealer," included the following, "The Federal Reserve told dealers it stood ready as a 'lender of last resort' to help banks meet 'unusual credit demands' related to the Drysdale situation."[5]

Meanwhile, *Real Clear Markets'* Randall Forsyth wrote about Drysdale in 2011. Forsyth noted that at the time of Drysdale's debacle 2-year Treasury interest rates were 14 percent. According to Forsyth, Drysdale would borrow Treasury securities with the highest accrued interest. Accrued interest would not be factored into the transaction. The thinking was because the tenor was so short, the interest rate didn't matter. [6]

Then, Drysdale would turn around and lend the Treasuries for a higher amount with the accrued interest factored in. The difference between the price sold plus the accrued interest helped bankroll Drysdale's position estimated to be around $4 billion.

On April 3, 2013, repo expert, Scott Skrym wrote about Drysdale's head of trading, David Heuwetter. "With years of declining bond markets, he had made a lot of money shorting the Treasury market and by February 1982 his trades reached $4.5 billion in short positions and $2.5 billion in long positions, as one Wall Street trader later remarked, 'It was the most astonishingly leveraged operation that I have ever seen.' Overall, it was not a bad trading strategy since he won under two out of three possible market scenarios. If the bond market went down, he made a lot of money. If the market stayed the same, he earned free interest on the cash the trade generated.

"If the Treasury market rallied, he risked a significant amount of money. As it turned out, between February 1982 and May 1982, the long end of the Treasury market rallied considerably."[7]

In his May 20, 1982, *New York Times* piece Michael Quint explained it this way, "In the Government securities businesses, volatility has become the byword in recent years and has encouraged the growth of short-term financing. For banks, the use of Treasury securities as collateral to arrange loans from businesses and others with spare cash to invest has been the fastest growing source of funds in recent years. Combining those borrowings with other overnight loans, large banks now roll over more than $100 billion of debt a day, up from $28 billion eight years ago."[8]

The repo market emerged without oversight. Its legitimacy as a business model was reinforced by the fact that the Federal Reserve had been engaging in repo transactions for some time. As stated, using repo, that is lending cash in exchange for securities to increase the money supply and reverse repo, which is lending securities for cash, to tighten the supply.

In 1983 the *New York Times* reported that Federal officials testifying before a senate subcommittee hearing said that the status of repo needed to be clarified and that in engaging in repo the Fed was sending a signal that is, an imprimatur which communicated to the financial industry it too, could engage in the practice.

And because there were scant regulations associated with the practice there were unforeseen consequences. Like no one considering whether accrued interest was being properly factored in when trading Treasuries.

At the time of the event, www.workers.org observed that "...the whole financial community knew only too well that the Drysdale affair signified profound economic and financial trouble. One would think, therefore, that with all the knowledge now available about the capitalist market in general, and the financial market in particular, immediate measures would have been taken (were that possible) to prevent a second inevitable shock wave.

"Wouldn't it be proper and in the self-interest of the so-called banking community to arrest another financial catastrophe? Wouldn't it be better to make private arrangements to prevent a domino effect in the financial markets than to have the government close the bank? Higher minds would think so, but this would by stymied by the very sharp and bitter competition among the banks themselves."[9]

According to a Jan. 31, 1983, article by the *New York Times'* Michael Quint the Federal Reserve was concerned about how failures like Drysdale could affect its use of repo as a monetary policy tool. Quint reported that Fed President Peter Sternlight said uncertainty surrounding Drysdale "could hamper the Fed's use of repo in monetary policy." [10]

I ask, couldn't the Fed restrict repo for its own use? Didn't the members see the handwriting on the wall? We are talking billions of dollars in the repo market of the 1980s. Small wonder it's in the trillions today.

Workers.org quotes economist and Columbia professor, Alfred Gaylord Hart in a story about Drysdale. His observations are prescient. "I fear this market is judged to be successful not on a record of integrity and responsibility but on the strength of its showing a huge volume of dealings, dealings which nobody understands but which enable some people to siphon off large gains from financial manipulations." (*New York Times* Letter May 31,1982.) [11]

Chase and Manufacturers Hanover paid the interest due at the urging of the Federal Reserve. Their stepping up allowed the repo government securities market to continue.

Several principals of Drysdale Securities were convicted of crimes. UPI reported extensively on the fallout in March 1985 sharing the offenses including "falsifying business records and fraudulently trading billions of dollars in government securities from 1976 to 1982."[12]

Following the Drysdale affair, it became standard practice to incorporate accrued interest as part of all Treasury transactions.

Chapter Three

LOMBARD WALL & SAFE HARBOR

"The safe harbors depart sharply from standard bankruptcy practice, effectively putting a large class of creditors outside the normal operation of the Code..."

---Edward R. Morrison, Mark J. Roe, Charles Evans Gerber & Christopher S. Sontchi

Three months after Drysdale, Lombard Wall Inc. and its subsidiary Lombard Wall Money Markets collapsed. The reason was that Bankers Trust, a clearing agent for the firm, refused to clear the trades, making it impossible for LW to operate and function normally.

Were it not for a knock-on effect from its bankruptcy filing Lombard-Wall would be relegated to a long list of failed forgotten businesses. Instead, it lives on in white papers, periodicals, and books.

Lombard Wall, it would turn out, would contribute to one of the most effective methods put in place to keep the repo market functioning. Or, as others view it, one of the most destructive pieces of bureaucratic interference in the history of the Street.

According to Robert J. Cole of the *New York Times* (Aug. 13, 1982) Lombard Wall had debts of $171 million and ten unsecured creditors, though he did not elaborate on the latter.

Cole quotes Bankers Trust's Thomas Parisis as saying that Lombard-Wall had provided his bank with financial data in March of 1982. This information, said Parisi, prompted "great concern."

Cole writes that several banks like Bankers Trust and Wall Street houses served as agents to "earn additional income."

As this case unfolded it became clear it involved repurchase agreements and in a rare instance repo is spoken of by a politician. This came by way of Ed Koch, the mayor of New York City. In a statement quoted by Cole, Koch said "...that two semiautonomous city agencies, in a move to collect 'maximum overnight interest' on their funds, had made so-called 'repurchase agreements' with Lombard - in effect lending money to Lombard with securities as a form of collateral."[1]

Yet another sign of things to come could be found in the Fed's signaling that it would be ready to lend to any institution with a problem, wrote Cole. Furthermore, he stated that this understanding was so entrenched that there would be no need for an "alert" by the Fed.

Because Lombard Wall blamed its troubles on interest rates one could speculate it had made some bad bets. Cole shared that with a trading volume of $500 million a day and limited capital invested an interest rate play could result in "sizable losses."

At issue in the bankruptcy proceedings was the automatic stay in the Bankruptcy Code. As defined on Investopedia: "The automatic stay is a provision in United States bankruptcy law that temporarily prevents creditors, collection agencies, government entities, and others from pursuing debtors for money that they owe."

A scholar who has tackled this topic is Carolyn Sissoko. Sissoko is affiliated with the University of the West of England. Her paper, "The Legal foundation of financial collapse" was published on the Social Sciences Research Network on Oct. 6, 2009. Here she addressed the ambiguity surrounding repo and the Bankruptcy Code.

"In 1982 when a small government securities dealer, Lombard Wall, declared bankruptcy, the bankruptcy judge found that Lombard Wall's repo contracts were secured loans. While the status of repos had been uncertain before, market participants in the past had held out the hope that 'friend of the court' briefs from the Federal Reserve and major investment banks would convince bankruptcy judges not to risk disrupting this huge market. Lombard Wall made it clear that some judges were not swayed by these arguments. Buyer-lenders in the repo market risked finding that collateral that had been pledged by a bankrupt firm had suddenly become a frozen asset, and, if the price of the collateral moved quickly, this illiquidity could lead to losses."[2]

Overseeing Lombard-Wall was Judge Edward J. Ryan of the U.S. Bankruptcy Court in Manhattan. Writing for the Yale Law Journal, Nathan Goralnik explained, "'Hoping to keep the wheels moving,' the bankruptcy judge later granted partial relief from the stay for many repo lenders, but he later recharacterized some of Lombard's repos as secured loans subject to the automatic stay.

"Thus, the Lombard-Wall bankruptcy frustrated the repo market's expectation that participants would enjoy immediate recourse to the cash (or securities) in their possession following a counterparty's default. The episode 'severely dislocated [the] financial markets,' and accelerated investors' post-Drysdale flight from the repo market." [3]

Meanwhile Jeanne L. Schroeder, Professor at Yeshiva University's Benjamin N. Cardozo School of Law wrote in her 2012 paper, "Repo Redo: Repurchase Agreements after the Real Estate Bubble," that "...the Fed was worried that treating repos as secured loans in bankruptcy would impede their use as tools for controlling the money supply." [4]

In 1984 Gary Walters wrote a paper for the Fordham Law Review. In it, he looked to Congress to address this situation.

Titled, "Repurchase Agreements and the Bankruptcy Code, the Need for Legislative Action," Walters underscores the threat of bankruptcy and how its attendant dictates were affecting the repo market. Wrote Walters, "Although it is difficult to isolate the impact of any single event in the financial markets some major institutions have left the market in response to the increased risk associated with a loan characterization. This trend toward market erosion has forestalled to some extent by the expectation that Congress will enact legislative relief." [5]

He continued, "If such legislation is not forthcoming more participants can be expected to leave the market," adding "The uncertain characterization of repo in the event of a participants bankruptcy has placed a cloud over the repo market."

Walters went on to say if nothing was done the consequences would be "severe," leading "to widespread bankruptcies of financial institutions and a collapse of government securities markets."

In his conclusion he stressed that "The critical financial importance of the repo market mandates legislation to exempt repo participants from the automatic stay."

Moving ahead to 1996 and a paper written by Jeanne Schroeder titled, "Repo Madness: The Characterization of Repurchase Agreements under the Bankruptcy Code and the U.C.C." (Universal Commercial Code). In it she tells us, "In 1984, Congress amended the Bankruptcy Code to assuage the repo industry, after the shock and heartache of Lombard Wall." [6]

Another term for the exemption from the automatic stay, is "safe harbor." In other words, the collateral on certain repo agreements would be protected from the fallout from a Chapter 11 filing. It would be for these agreements, "business as usual."

It is important to note that in the 1984 provision, protected collateral was relegated to Treasury securities, Bankers' Acceptance,

Certificates of Deposit and Government Agency securities. The thinking was these securities were fungible and would therefore be easily dispensed within the functioning repo market. Schroeder explains the rationale, the automatic stay exemption, she writes, would allow "the repo market to maintain its primary function of providing liquidity in the markets." In other words, it would "Keep repo running smoothly, without disruption."[7]

In it she retraces the history of safe harbor. Saying that before repo it had been granted under certain provisions regarding the trading of commodities. An important distinction is made that prior to the dispensation given the repo market, any safe harbor protection was always done in conjunction with a regulatory body overseeing the respective market involved.

Not so, with repo. Carolyn Sissoko writes in her paper, "The 1984 law set a precedent for the expansion of safe harbor to unregulated financial contracts. The repo amendment to the Bankruptcy Code had established the principle that the imprimatur of a self-regulatory organization was not necessary for a financial contract to receive safe harbor."[8]

As it turns out the 1984 amendment would be just the beginning.

Sissoko references the 1998 collapse of Long-Term Capital.* She writes the collapse, "shed light on shortcomings of safe harbor provisions. Not all contracts fit the qualifying definition, and this made for a messy cleanup."[9]

Then writes Sissoko, in 2005 the Bankruptcy Act "broadened the safe harbor protections granted contracts so they would all be uniform."[10] The enormity of this topic is stunning.

It wasn't until a second or even third reading of Sissoko's paper that I came to understand safe harbor was expanded to virtually all financial contracts, including securities contracts, commodities contracts, forward contracts, repo and swaps. [11]

Sissoko says, "After 2005 any right negotiated bilaterally in a securities contract

*Long-Term Capital Management was a large hedge fund, led by Nobel-prize winning economists and renowned Wall Street traders, that blew up in 1998. Ultimately the U.S. government had to step in and arrange a bailout of LTCM by a consortium of Wall Street banks in order to prevent systemic contagion".
—Investopedia

securities contract was redefined to include the purchase and sale of residential mortgages was granted safe harbor and the term and repurchase agreements on stocks, bonds, and mortgages. These changes granted safe harbor to huge swathes of over-the-counter transactions that had never had this protection including cash CDOs, mortgage-backed securities and repurchase agreements on securities contracts. The breadth of the definitions made it easy to develop new financial products that would also be protected from the bankruptcy code."[12]

Sissoko observes, "The fact that the biggest players in the financial industry will be able to exempt whatever transactions they so choose from bankruptcy is apparently acceptable to Congress."[13]

Sissoko postures that safe harbor provides "a false sense of security." She writes, "After all easy risk management may induce firms to feel comfortable with lower levels of equity capital, thus reducing the firms' ability to survive adverse events. In short, easy risk management may increase rather than decrease systemic risk."[14]

And when it comes to regulators, Sissoko says they "justify the bankruptcy exemptions by deploying an implicit model which posits a linear relationship between credit losses at financial institutions and systemic risk – without explaining the foundations of their belief in this relationship.

"Instead, the regulators simply assume that if they can keep the banks from experiencing losses, they will be addressing systemic risk."[15]

She points out that one cannot escape the fact that the market blew up just three years after these expanded safe harbor allowances were enacted.

"Rolling Back the Repo Safe Harbors" was written in 2014. Its authors were Edward R. Morrison, Charles Evans Gerber Professor of Law at Columbia Law School, Mark J. Roe, a David Berg Professor of Corporate Law at Harvard Law School, and Christopher S. Sontchi, United States Bankruptcy Judge for the District of Delaware.

In it they state, "Special rules exempt an increasingly wide arc of creditors from the normal operation of bankruptcy.

These so-called 'safe harbors' exempt the bankrupt debtor's financial-contract counterparties from the basic rules that halt creditor collection efforts when the bankruptcy begins, that claw back preferential and fraudulent pre-bankruptcy transfers that harm creditors overall, and that facilitate orderly liquidation or reorganization. These safe harbors for financial contracts exist for one articulated purpose: to promote stability in financial markets.

"Yet there is no evidence that they serve this purpose. Instead, considerable evidence shows that, when they matter most—in a financial crisis—the safe harbors exacerbate the crisis, weaken critical financial institutions, destabilize financial markets, and then prove costly to the real economy." [16]

Case in point, writing for the Banking Law Journal in 2015 about Title II of Dodd-Frank, Paul L. Lee shares the observations of the late Harvey Miller, the lead bankruptcy attorney for Lehman Bros.[9] Miller, he wrote, "testified that the exclusion from the Bankruptcy Code's automatic stay for derivatives, swap, and other securities transactions had caused a 'massive destruction' of value for Lehman. In his words, the exclusions in the Bankruptcy Code exposed Lehman to the 'ravages of counterparties' in respect of its securities and structured finance contracts."

Lee further states that, "Some experts had warned even before the Lehman bankruptcy that the special treatment for financial contracts could be a source of systemic risk in a bankruptcy proceeding of a large financial institution." [17]

Morrison, Roe, Gerber and Sontchi also point out another offshoot of the exemption which is not good for the wider world. According to them, "The best available evidence...shows that the safe harbors distort the capital structure decisions of financial firms by subsidizing runnable short-term financing at the expense of other, safer debt channels, including longer-term financing. When financial firms favor volatile short-term over more stable long-term debt, they (and markets generally) are more likely to experience a 'run' in the event of a market shock such as the downturn in housing prices during our most recent recession."[18]

The long and the short of it is, the trio say, "It is time for the Bankruptcy Code to get out of the business of regulating financial markets." Well, not entirely. They seek a return to the 1984 safe harbors "for agreements involving United States Treasury securities and several other highly liquid assets (e.g., bank certificates of deposit, eligible bankers' acceptances, and agency securities backed by the government full faith and credit.)."

And yes, exemptions from the automatic stay were/are inextricably tied to shadow banking. As written in "Rolling Back the Repo Safe Harbors," "The safe harbors played an important role in the growth of shadow banking. Corporate cash managers, as well as pension and mutual funds, investment banks, and other institutional investors with large cash reserves want immediate access to this cash but would also like to earn a return on the cash until it is needed. Safe-harbored repos provide the solution..." [19]

Earlier in this chapter the Uniform Commercial Code *was cited in the title by Jeanne Schroeder.

According to www.uniformlaws.org, "The Uniform Commercial Code (UCC) is a comprehensive set of laws governing all commercial transactions in the United States. It is not a federal law, but a uniformly adopted state law. Uniformity of law is essential in this area for the interstate transaction of business."

On reading the paper the U.C.C. reference eluded me, and I gave it no thought. That was a mistake. And while Schroeder's paper didn't ring any alarm bells, recently I have come to learn of the U.C.C.'s role in safe harbor and the alarm bells are ringing loud and clear.

In his 2023 book, "The Great Taking," David Rogers Webb explains the implications of the U.C.C. and its role in the dissolution of financial institutions. According to Webb, over the years, the U.C.C. has been amended in all 50 states. Quietly and stealthily, the U.C.C. has codified a legal concept. "Security Entitlement" is now accorded investors like you and me. And what that means is that in the event of bankruptcy secured creditors, those who manage our assets and according to Webb use them as collateral have priority over accountholders when it comes to disbursement of those assets. [20]

Here he explains his first encounter with this phenomenon, "I had expected widespread failures of financial institutions and had watched closely for the first signs. In 2008, I noticed the failure of a small broker dealer in Florida, and I was shocked to learn that client assets owned outright with no borrowing against them were swept to the receiver and encumbered in the bankruptcy estate.

"I had to understand how this could possibly have happened, and eventually uncovered that ownership right to securities, which had been personal property for four centuries, had somehow been subverted. This would be born out further in the bankruptcies of Lehman Brothers and MF Global."[21]

Yes, safe harbor is about exemption from the automatic stay. What I failed to grasp was just how the residual assets are distributed. I failed to understand that in concert with safe harbor is the erasure of our property rights.

You will read more about Mr. Webb in Chapter Ten of this book.

Repo expert Scott Skyrm observed, "Imagine if the judge had ruled that Repo was technically a collateralized loan and the Repo financing was therefore tied up in bankruptcy court potentially for years. There would clearly be no 'shadow banking' industry without the ability to quickly liquidate Repo trades in the event of a bankruptcy."[22]

Chapter Four

COLLATERAL

"In many ways, collateral has become the new cash, underpinning the smooth functioning of funding and capital markets, and, in turn, providing the basis for economic growth."

--European Repo Council 2014

There would be no repo without collateral. Collateral is tied to each repo. Like the song, "Love and Marriage," you can't have one without the other.

Returning to the image of the ball of twine enveloping the earth, imagine that all these financial transactions traveling through our fiber optic transom are not one but two as in the second "leg" of a repo, which is providing the collateral for the cash lent. The lending is the first "leg." And in the case of reverse repo, the first leg is the "lending" of securities, and the second the acquisition of cash collateral.

What makes it even more complicated is the fact that the same collateral may be used to support multiple transactions.

Here is an excerpt from a Dec. 21, 2018, Federal Reserve Bank of New York paper titled "The Ins and Outs of Collateral Re-Use:" "...the free circulation of collateral comes at a cost. Namely, the re-use of collateral increase interconnectedness and can contribute to fragility in financial markets by increasing the uncertainty regarding who holds the collateral, the ability of counterparties to return the collateral, and who is entitled to the collateral in case of default. The use and re-use of collateral can create long 'collateral chains' in which one security is used for multiple transactions. These collateral chains have the potential to propagate uncertainties and amplify fragility in times of market stress."[1]

Mary Fricker put it this way as part of her 2012 presentation previously cited. "In a repurchase agreement, companies use securities as collateral to get a loan from another shadow banker, often just overnight. At this step something interesting happens. In a securities lending transaction or in a repurchase transaction, somebody gives cash and gets back securities. Whoever gets the securities can re-use the same securities as collateral to get a repo loan for themselves. And so on.

"This creates a daisy chain, where the same securities become collateral for several loans. It's called "rehypothecation," and it's another reason that shadow banking is so interconnected."[2]

There are myriad firms throughout the globe dedicated to collateral use. Terms like the "collateral highway," "collateral optimization," "fluidity," abound. Among issues raised in financial institutions is that of collateral coordination. Oftentimes you will see references to a central clearing platform which could track all collateral movement. This raises concerns about concentration risk.

Sunguard's April 2015 "Collateralization Optimization: The Next Generation of Collateral Management," states at the outset, "The post-crisis banking regime has obliged financial institutions to make connections between previously distinct classes of risk. The traditional view of a sequential flow of risk has been replaced by an *infinite, interconnected loop* with collateral and liquidity at the center alongside risk-weighted assets." (My italics) (According to Investopedia risk-weighted assets are "used to determine the minimum amount of capital that must be held by banks and other financial institutions to reduce the risk of insolvency. The capital requirement is based on a risk assessment for each type of bank asset.)[3]

There you have it, an "interconnected, infinite loop." Within this loop are maneuverers whose sole purpose is to ensure the markets run smoothly. Among them the Depository Trust and Clearing Corporation whose mission is to provide clearing and settlement services for the financial markets.

The DTCC's website states, "Repo transactions are processed, compared, and netted along with other government securities trades each day by the Government Securities Division (GSD) of DTCC's Fixed Income Clearing Corporation (FICC) as part of its business of handling of all the post-trade processing in the trillion-dollar market for government securities.

"Included in this repo service is an automated facility that supports the substitution of repo collateral. To make use of the facility, participants must follow an established set of rules governing how substitution information should be communicated to FICC and when substitute collateral must be made available."[4]

The DTCC is privately owned by banks and brokers. According to Wikipedia "In 2011, DTCC settled the vast majority of securities transactions in the United States and close to $1.7 *quadrillion* in value worldwide, making it by far the highest financial value processor in the world." (my italics).

We all know that leading up to the financial crisis was a crisis in collateral. A lot of it was bad so sell-offs began.

In his 2013 article "Repo, Baby, Repo," writing for Counterpunch, Mark Whitney said, "What touched off the crash of 2008 was the discovery that the collateral that was being used for repo funding was 'toxic,' that is the securities were not Triple A after all, but subprime mortgage-backed junk, which would only fetch pennies on the dollar."[5]

Whitney continues, "The point is had the system been adequately regulated with the appropriate safeguards in place there would have been no fire sales, no panic, and no crisis.

"Regulation would have made sure that the underlying collateral was legit, that is, they have to be sure that the subprime borrowers were creditworthy and able to repay their loans. They would have made sure that repo-borrowers (the banks) had sufficient capital to meet redemptions if problems arose and regulation would have limited excessive leverage."

"Regulation works," he concluded.

I came across the following observation on a blog called Alhambria. Writing in 2014 in the Contra Corner, Jeffrey Snider said, "The money supply right now is no such thing as money has vanished from banking. Liquidity itself is not dependent on 'money supply' so much as the means and channels for *flow*. That was the lesson learned the hard way by those that assured everyone in 2007 that all was contained." (my italics)[6]

Snider then pointed out the Fed's Reverse Repo Facility as a way to "live up to the elasticity in the real 'currency' of the modern bank-*collateral*." (my italics)

International Capital Markets Association analyst Richard Comotto tells us in a May 2013 paper titled, "A supplementary note on the systemic importance of collateral and role of the repo market," that "Collateralization to hedge credit risk and liquidity risk is central to the current global regulatory framework, the only alternative is a public guarantee explicit or implicit."[7]

In April of 2014, the New York Fed published a report, "Mixing and Matching Collateral in Dealer Banks." It was written by four staffers: Adam Kirk, James McAndrews, Parinitha Sastry and Phillip Weed. It begins, "In some ways dealer banks resemble well-understood traditional banks which use deposits they receive from savers to make loans for businesses and households. Unlike traditional banks however dealer banks rely on complex and unique collateralized borrowing and lending, which often involves the simultaneous exchange of cash and securities with other large and sophisticated institutions."[8]

Furthermore, it is important to note, in "normal times such transactions are highly efficient for allocating scarce resources," Scarce resources?" The allusion to "scarce resources" gave me pause. And then I got to thinking perhaps there is not enough collateral to support individual transactions hence the need to repledge. The next sentence was crystal clear, "During times of stress they have proven to be 'destabilizing.'"

Now, let's see about leverage for those of us who do not understand these institutions, you know, these sophisticated institutions.

Admittedly, I am not doing a deep dive into regulatory matters. But in this instance let's look at where it stands today. A website named efinancemanagment.com explains how we, the public, can become ensnared within this market without even knowing it.[9] "The US, Federal Reserve Regulation T and SEC

Rule 15c3-3 allows the broker rehypothecation of collateral submitted by the clients to the extent of 140% of the loan amount extended."

An example provided describes when an investor buys $500 worth of stock A. Not having enough money to purchase Stock B, he borrows $500 using Stock A as collateral. This transaction then allows the dealer to re-pledge $700 as collateral in other unrelated transactions.

The unnamed explainer continues, "The frightening part is that such rehypothecation can occur without even as much as an intimation to us. Yes, the brokers and financial institutions are authorized to rehypothecate our assets without notifying us. Apparently, such clauses are part of the fine print of the agreement we sign while opening an account with them. In effect, we ourselves give consent to our own doom when we sign those papers."

The final section of the previously cited FRBNY 2014 piece is aptly titled "Unique and Complex Risks." In it they conclude by referring to the practice of collateral substitution saying, "Finding a substitute at equivalent cost can be difficult in an illiquid market." Failure to find collateral matching

Client A's position would result in "damage to a dealer's reputation." And then some...

The next telling observation comes at the end where they compare a world of collateral versus non-collateral stating, "Furthermore the efficiencies gained from dealer banking should be weighed against the *social cost* that accompany a systemic risk event. Further research on the role that dealer banks play in securities markets should shed some light on such tradeoffs."[10] (my italics)

One can only conclude that referencing "social cost" is disingenuous at best. Clearly "further research" is a throwaway line, indicating that our role or lack thereof has yet to warrant a closer look. Meanwhile, the vulnerabilities remain.

Take this excerpt from a European Commission report as reported by *Bloomberg's* Jim Brunsden and John Glover in August 2013. "Complex chains of collateral can make it difficult for investors to identify who owns what, where risk is concentrated and who is exposed to whom." The report continued, "This has consequences for transparency and financial stability."[11]

I harken back to Carolyn Sissoko's 2009 paper "The legal foundations of financial collapse" where she writes "Recent experience indicates, however, that the special treatment granted to repurchase agreements and over the counter derivatives tends to reduce the stability of the financial system by encouraging collateralized interbank lending and discouraging careful analysis of the credit risk of counterparties."[12]

I conclude this chapter with a ring side seat at a 2016 collateral brainstorming session. It came by way of a transcript I stumbled upon.

Attendees covered the spectrum including representatives from major financial institutions, collateral management companies and to round it out a software developer.

The participant from the collateral management firm set the tone. "Our priorities in collateral management are primarily to grow the connectivity that we have on the Collateral Highway, in terms of both sourcing and delivering both bonds and equities from around the world on behalf of our clients. Equally, we must be able to allocate such securities collateral to an ever-expanding ecosystem of collateral receivers, liquidity providers and risk mitigators. There are exit or delivery points on the Collateral Highway."

He goes on to say that exits on the Collateral Highway include the central banks ("key exit points"). Also included are the clearing platforms in place-- "day to day" business involves bringing new liquidity providers onto the Highway, whether they are corporate cash providers, insurance companies, securities lenders, or commercial banks."

Over the next several pages one finds a spirited discussion about collateral and how it is dispensed across the board. New regulations are discussed and their impact on the "highway." At one point the man representing the software firm, says, "In terms of infrastructure, the challenge of the industry is providing a sufficient engine for unlocking collateral supply and matching it with demand."

Further on, he observes, "In the longer term maybe a change in derivative trading will evolve. Perhaps we could even see collateral turning into a *derivative in its own right.* So, you could take out a contract for a future delivery of Central Clearing Platform eligible collateral on a given date...and that will mean they don't necessarily have to hold those assets until they are delivered." (My italics). Pointing out the current situation, a participant representing a major financial institution commented "Clearly, there is a massive education of the clients and a massive infrastructure development investment within the bank. To reiterate everyone's points---it is a massive problem to solve...Being able to solve the impact of certain stress scenarios, you need all of that technology on the secure financing side across all the sources and all of the requirements of that collateral." In other words, "It's complicated."

Chapter Five

REPO'S COUSIN

"...much of the demand for borrowing results from short
selling related to a whole host of other trading strategies
including convertible arbitrage, warrant arbitrage, risk
arbitrage, options trading and long/short strategies."

--Leslie S. Nelson
Retired Goldman Sachs Managing Director

A slow boat to China took me to securities lending. An area that I found among the most intimidating in my journey through the financial mazes.

In her previously mentioned presentation, Mary Fricker cites repo and securities lending as the two main ways to conduct shadow banking.[1]

According to the Financial Oversight Committee's 2021 Annual Report, "Securities lending transactions involve the temporary transfer of a security by one party (the lender) to another (the borrower) in exchange for cash or non-cash collateral."

Like repo securities lending involves lending securities for cash collateral. According to the 2013 Federal Reserve Bank of New York paper "Repo and Securities Lending," "In the United States most securities lending is done against cash collateral. Typically, the lender of a security pays an interest rate to the borrower for the cash collateral."[2]

Again, the provider of collateral is called the counterparty-just like repo.

At a Sept. 29. 2009 roundtable conducted by the Securities and Exchange Commission on securities lending, Chairman, Mary Schapiro referenced its history, "Securities lending has existed in some parts of the world since at least the 19th century, if not earlier. In the 1970s, securities lending increased in the U.S. as custodian banks lent out the portfolio securities of their custodial clients, and registered investment companies began lending their securities. In the 1990s and early 2000s, with the expansion of the global securities markets and investing, and the exponential increase in short selling and related strategies, the demand for securities lending also grew."[3]

According to the FRBNY paper, "Repo and Securities Lending," the main lenders of securities are called "beneficial asset holders." They are comprised of pension funds, mutual funds, hedge funds and insurance companies." [4]

Why do they lend out securities? "To enhance yield," says the Fed. "Because borrowing securities is mainly used for short-selling, derivative hedging or avoiding 'fails,' the main borrowers are hedge funds, asset managers, option traders and market makers." Meanwhile, the cash collateral is also used to generate miniscule returns that add up to real money.

A sampling of what kinds of activities the borrowers may be up to is revealed in a 2015 paper published by the Securities Finance Trust Company. Titled, "Securities Lending Best Practices" it includes this description of a strategy which may be employed. It is called "share class arbitrage" and according to the paper, "Discrepancies between prices of a company listed on more than one exchange and/or different classes of securities trading on the same exchange. The borrower will sell short the security with the higher price and purchase the security with the lower price in the expectation that the gap will eventually close." [5]

Here's another example it is called "Dividend yield enhancement." The paper states, "Discrepancies between the net dividend received by the beneficial owner in different markets. The borrower will take the shares from a lender required to pay withholding tax on a dividend and transfer the shares to a beneficial owner subject to less, or no withholding tax. The lender is essentially able to receive a higher dividend in the form of additional securities lending revenue, than if the security remained in custody."

Because hedge funds are the major players, the paper explains that lenders rarely work directly with them. The reasons cited are that hedge funds "are unlikely to have the required collateral as the prime broker sources it for them." And "The lending agent appointed by the lender will typically indemnify or protect the lender against a borrower default. As hedge funds are generally smaller and less capitalized entities."

Examples of lending agents may be found in an undated Deutsche Bank publication titled "Deutsche Funds Securities Lending Overview."[6]

Deutsche lists three "lending agents' as part of its program. They are Brown Brothers Harriman, Deutsche Bank Agency Lending and State Street Bank and Trust.

And while indemnification is somehow comparable to an insurance policy, concerns have been raised by the Financial Stability Board that indemnification itself potentially could be a source of instability, writing in its 2017 report "Policy Recommendations to Address Structural Vulnerabilities from Asset Management Activities," that "If most securities lenders would not engage in securities lending absent such a guarantee, an impairment of the value of this indemnification commitment could lead lenders to withdraw suddenly from the market."[7]

Meanwhile a walk over to the Deutsche Bank's website reveals that as of March 31, 2022, 22 of its mutual funds engage in securities lending including the DWS Equity 500 Index Fund and DWS Global Bond Fund. [8] And just how are the revenues from securities lending dispensed? Are they passed on to investors or retained by financial institutions?

The answer is embedded in, yet another issue raised when it comes to sec lending.

According to a recent submission to the Securities and Exchange Commission the Americans for Financial Reform Education Fund addressed what it views as a conflict of interest when it comes to deciding whether to recall shares for sec lending or maintain shares that allow for voting rights. "There is not much public information about how asset managers allocate revenues from securities lending; therefore, it is difficult to know the extent to which individual investors are or are not benefiting from securities lending revenues, and how those benefits would compare to what they could be gaining from proxy voting. However, it has been reported that one asset management company passes 70% of these revenues to investors and retains the rest, potentially tilting the scale in favor of revenues from securities lending and against recalling shares to vote."9

One asset company? So that fact is that we have no idea whether clients are benefitting from securities lending or not. Giving the lie to Standards Board of Alternative Investments' 2022 declaration in an SEC submission that securities lending, "provides a source of income to institutional investors."

Of course, all of this is automated with the Deposit Trust and Clearing Corporation playing a pivotal role. And just like with the collateral highway there are myriad firms devoted to tracking the sec lending market.

The Securities Finance Trust Company's "Best Practices" paper states that "Substantial transparency into securities lending activity currently exists as a result of services provided by organizations such as Markit

Securities Finance, SunGard Astec Analytics and DataLend."[10] I traveled to the DataLend website and was greeted by this pronouncement: "October 2021 Securities Lending Revenue Up 34% YoY to $821 million."[11]

Also on the site was a description of their strategy that left me breathless! "We scan our universe of more than 42,000 securities on loan to find those securities with the most expensive financing positions in the U.S., the U.K., Europe and Asia. Financing costs are determined by taking the total on loan value of a security and multiplying it by volume-weighted average fees to borrow that security, then converting the product of those numbers to a dollar value. We then sort the most expensive securities to finance in the securities lending market in descending order." Whew!

On the DataLend homepage you will see that as of April 2021 $28.9 trillion was "lendable." Trillion lent was $2.75 and securities on loan during that month totaled "58,000+."

Another offshoot of the sec lending marketplace are companies whose purpose is to track counterparty credit risk.

Interos is one such firm. Here's what is says on its website, "Instant visibility into your supply chain. A breakthrough SaaS platform that uses artificial intelligence to model the total ecosystems of complex businesses into a living global map, down to any single supplier, anywhere."[12]

S&P Global Market Intelligence pledges to "Streamline your counterparty credit risk assessment with RiskGauge. These detailed business credit reports are powered by dynamic analytical models and extensive private company data and are available for over 50 million public and private companies across the globe—including small- and medium-enterprises (SMEs)."[13]

And of course, there are those firms whose sole purpose is to provide information on what stocks to short. This is a market not without controversy. Here is an instant where it ran afoul.

Reported by Reuters on June 22, 2021, "A small Texas investor who caused shares of a real estate investment trust to plunge 39 percent in a day has agreed to pay the company restitution to settle a lawsuit against him, a rare development that could embolden other companies to pursue such claims."[14]

Quinton Mathews, who published his research on companies online under the pseudonym Rota Fortunae, will pay Farmland Partners Inc (FPI.N) 'a multiple' of the profits on his short bet in 2018, according to the terms of the legal settlement announced late Sunday. His research had helped wipe as much as $115 million off Farmland's market value.

Mathews conceded that "many of the key statements in a report - including allegations of dubious related-party transactions and the risk of insolvency - were wrong." Oops!

And it just so happens I am writing this on the heels of a Dec. 10, 2021, Bloomberg article titled, "Hedge Funds Face Expansive Short-Selling Probe, Exciting Critics." The first paragraph states, "The U.S. Justice Department has launched an expansive criminal investigation into short selling by hedge funds and research firms -- thrilling legions of small investors and other skeptics of the tactics that investigative firms use to bet on stock declines."[15]

Meanwhile, claims of sec lending transparency by myriad firms servicing the sector apparently fall short. This is evidenced in a 2012 article by Josh Galper of Finadium that echoes the push for a Legal Entity

Identifier and the BIS's call for "simple, transparent and comparable securitizations."

In his article, "Intraday Securities Lending Data and a Securities Lending Ticker." Galper wrote, "The possibility of such a ticker for securities loans on how data can be standardized." Then, he proceeds to qualify his thesis, "Some form of standardized securities lending may be closer to equity or options data...This would not be the same as analyzing the full securities lending market." He concludes "The potential for intraday securities lending data to be transformed into a ticker is enticing to regulators particularly regulators who are new to the securities lending arena. This is an interesting path and one that is almost certain to lead to errors and confusion without product standardization.[14] With a standardized and cleaned up feed however, a new opportunity emerges for a wide range of market participants." [16]

That was back in 2012 and in 2021 the SEC proposed Rule 10c-1. Its purpose: to provide transparency in the securities lending market which according to Commissioner Gary Gensler is "opaque." [17] So, I guess for almost 10 years the sec lending market has been fraught with "errors and confusion."

Simultaneously the SEC is seeking comments on, yet another rule aimed at taming the tiger. This one has to do with short-selling transparency. It is Rule 13f-2[18]. Both Rules have garnered hundreds of comments though interestingly, the lion's share of comments on short-selling are from everyday folks while many of the sec-lending commentaries originate from large institutions and associations.

Both rule changes emanate from Section 984-B of Dodd-Frank about market transparency. In my opinion it is a hot mess.

There is much discussion about the overlapping of securities lending and short selling. After all securities lending "enables short-selling," according to the comment submitted by the Standards Board for Alternative investments.

How to differentiate? How to parse? The idea that blurring the label of repos with sec lending to evade reporting requirements is another area of concern raised. It's endless. We are more than 10 years out from Dodd-Frank and still huge swaths of the market are out of view. I am not naïve. I know all of this is integral to the ongoing financial health of companies that have nothing to do with Wall Street. This is evident in the following quote from the Financial Stability Oversight Council, published in 2020. "The fall in assets in March 2020 led to deleveraging by market participants that typically borrow securities, and the lower asset prices and lower demand for new securities lending in general reduced the amount of cash collateral reinvested in the short-term funding markets. This deleveraging limited the supply of capital available in the STFMs, making it difficult for issuers in the real economy to access capital."[19]

I don't care. I see repos, sec-lending and short-selling as akin the Gorgons of Greek Mythology. The transactions are like the living, venomous snakes that adorned their heads and they had it within their power to turn people to stone. We, you, and me, are the stones; pebbles trod upon by the endless, time-wasting, resource devouring shadow banking system.

Finally, the structure of securities lending transactions begs the question, are they too exempt from the automatic stay under the Bankruptcy Code?

Turns out they are. A 2014 research paper published by the law firm Hunton & Williams, now Hunton Andrews Kurth, addresses the subject.[20]

Written by J.R. Smith, Anthony Pijertov and Justin Paget, "Sailing Without Headwind: Structured Lending Market Embraces Bankruptcy Safe Harbor Provisions," states the following, "Repurchase agreements and securities contract safe harbor structures dominate the U.S. market, permitting lenders to exercise remedies largely free from intervening Bankruptcy proceedings that add costs and delay lender recoveries."

The paper traces several court cases and reaches the following conclusion, "The push to qualify ordinary financial transactions as safe harbor contracts has met with little resistance from the courts. One seeming result is a shifting of the burden in U.S. bankruptcies from lenders and other providers of capital who can avail themselves of safe harbor provisions to other creditors, such as trade vendors...In the absence of any trend-reversing decisions from the circuit courts, or an unlikely decision from the U.S. Supreme Court, Congress ultimately will need to consider whether safe harbor provisions still serve the role it initially intended."

Chapter Six

CURRENT ISSUES

"In other words, using the cash as a source of financial leverage means it no longer serves as a purely risk-mitigation function."

--Frank M. Keane

I was constantly challenged each time I read a report about any aspect of the shadow banking system. One such report was published by the New York Fed. It was just one of many published under the moniker "Current Issues." When I read it, my reaction was the usual, to freeze up as if to say to myself "You are not going to understand this, so why bother reading it." Then, I thought I would focus on this one report. And read it several times over until I did get it or at least most of it.

"Current Issues" was a series of publications by the New York Fed that ran from 1997 to 2014. During 2013 seven reports were released and the one I focused on was by a man named Frank M. Keane. *Current Issues Vol. 19, Nov. 3*, was titled, "Securities Loans, Collateralized by Cash: Reinvestment Risk, Run Risk, and Incentive Issues."[1]

In this chapter, I am sharing Mr. Keane's report. Why? Because of the very fact that it is one of millions of reports written on the financial markets. I guess, my intent is to give a taste of what's out there. What's being written and analyzed and absorbed by people we don't know. People who, no doubt, populate that exclusive club up the road. It is just one tiny, tiny cog in the massive machine called shadow banking.

So, think about this while you are eating your cereal in the morning and going off to a job that has nothing to do with Wall Street. Think about those people who are forever trying to turn straw into gold. And sometimes they do. Take this paper where Mr. Keane is troubled by a practice which allows agents to have an unfair advantage.

To review. Hedge funds, broker-dealers and portfolio managers routinely borrow securities. The lenders of the securities are known as the "beneficial owners" and according to Keane include insurance companies, pension funds, mutual funds, and banks. The latter enlist the services of an "agent-lender." This role is carried out by "the custodian for the beneficial owner of the securities, by an internal business function within the beneficial owner or by an independent entity."

Keane explains that the "beneficial owner" can make money in two ways. One, a fee it's paid for lending the security and two, the returns earned on cash collateral reinvestment. At the same time, he writes that the lender pays the borrower a rate on the cash collateral! It's called a rebate rate. Keane points to a relationship between the value of the security and the rebate rate. The more desirable a security the lower the rebate rate. So, says Keane, a high rebate rate could be more indicative of a securities lender needing to borrow cash than the borrower needing to lend the security.

Keane's paper addresses the issue of agents reinvesting cash collateral in risky investments. "Riskier and more illiquid assets will typically offer a higher potential yield. Comparing the cash reinvestment rate with prevailing money market rates of return offers some indication of the relative risk of the reinvestment activity."

And, when gains are from these transactions they are split between the agent and the "beneficial owner" that is, the entity that lent the security. However, if this cash reinvestment activity results in loss, the agent-lender does not share in the loss leaving, Keane writes, the beneficial owner "fully exposed to unsuccessful investment strategies." Thus, Keane writes, this structure "provides the agent with an incentive to pursue high-risk investment strategies."

Addressing the logistics of these arrangements Keane observes that "An important consequence of making the main purpose of a securities loan the generation of cash in support of an aggressive reinvestment strategy is that the role of cash as collateral may be compromised. In other words, using the cash as a source of financial leverage means it no longer serves as a purely risk-mitigation function. Instead, the cash now becomes a source of liquidity and financial risk."

And says Keane if you think this behavior is inconsequential; just a tiny corner of the immensely complex financial ecosystem, think again. "AIG used this form of securities lending as a mechanism for raising cash to support a yield-enhancement reinvestment strategy with no collateral market purpose..."

Continuing, "In AIG's case, liquidity and financial risk related to cash reinvestment that rose to a level that threatened the survival of the institution and financial stability more generally.

"Understandably, on the heels of these events came calls for greater transparency in securities lending."

Keane writes, "The open-ended nature of cash reinvestment...have, in some cases, resulted in cash reinvestment well beyond the relative safety of money market investments, stretching maturity and credit transformation to imprudent and unsustainable levels."

Finally, he says, "While it might be tempting to suggest eliminating the lending of securities against cash collateral, such a policy response may be too extreme." Why? Because "some uses of the practice are benign. It does, for example make it easier to intermediate between repo and securities-lending transactions in sourcing specific securities for collateral market transactions." And he continues, "...cash reinvestment activities are for the most part, managed appropriately."

Ultimately, he calls for data transparency. This, he says, would be a "reasonable cost" to avert "runs" and the "risk of financial system disruption."

I have emailed the FRBNY several times to inquire as to whether the agent advantage has been addressed. And each time I have been met with radio silence.

In sum, this paper is but one nugget, one tiny little speck on the landscape that is shadow banking and its attendant analyses by the New York Fed, academics, etc. What would they do with their time if they didn't have this to write about? And don't forget, students of economics are not even privy to this stuff. At least not at the college where my neighbor's daughter-in-law teaches.

Part II

What About Us?"

Chapter Seven

TAKING STOCK

"Fairness is the heart of the Rule of Law."

---Edward J. Kane

On July 31, 2014, Boston College professor of Finance, Edward J. Kane testified before the Financial Institutions and Consumer Protection subcommittee of the U.S. Senate Committee on Banking and Urban Affairs.

His presentation was titled, "Statement on Measuring the Funding Advantages Enjoyed by Large, Complex, and Politically Powerful Bank Holding Companies."[1]

This was his opening sentence, "I want to begin by thanking Chairman Brown (U.S. Senator Sherrod Brown (D-Ohio), for inviting me to testify today and to congratulate him and the Subcommittee for continuing to battle against the *pernicious* and unfair advantage that panic-driven crisis management policies confer on mega-institutions not only in this country but in financial center countries around the world." (My italics) He didn't stop there, "The idea that the Dodd-Frank Act of

2010 or Basel III can end the advantages is a dangerous pipe dream."

Kane's testimony is predicated on the belief that for all intent and purposes Too Big To Fail or TBTF institutions have an inbuilt guarantee that were trouble to arise the authorities would step up and bail the firm out. He testified that, "This inarticulate backstop means lower credit risk as reflected in more attractive rates. This leads to a lower cost of debt which in turn, buttresses the stock price. Or as Kane put it himself this is a "contra-liability provided by an unlimited guarantee."

Kane continued with this observation, "Bailout funding can more accurately be described as unbalanced equity investments...The government's bailout deals compare very unfavorably with the deal Warren Buffet negotiated in rescuing Goldman-Sachs. Buffet's deal carried a running yield of 10 percent and included warrants* that gave him substantial claim on Goldman's future profits."

*Warrants are a derivative that give the right, but not the obligation, to buy or sell a security—most commonly an equity—at a certain price before expiration. The price at which the underlying security can be bought or sold is referred to as the exercise price or strike price.

Furthermore, he stated the government chose its path "without weighing the full range of out-of-pocket and implicit costs of their rescue programs against the costs and benefits of alternative programs such as prepackaged bankruptcies or temporary nationalization." (See Bair 2012).

How do these mega institutions manage to keep this arrangement in play? Kane answers the question, "A firm account to senators and congresspersons grows steadily and with it a geographical footprint with a number of employees that can be persuaded to contribute to re-election campaigns. TBTF Bank Holding Companies or BHCs give heavily to candidates in both political parties as Ferguson, Jorgenson and Chen (2013) have documented.

"Holding size constant, the more organizationally complex and politically influential an institution becomes the better the chance that government examiners will find it difficult to observe its exposure to tail risk and to discipline such risk adequately."

During his testimony, he addressed the shortcomings of the bailouts, telling the Subcommittee that, "Regulators and policy makers persistently mis-frame bail out expenditures as either loans or insurance.

This false characterization helps TBTF firms and their creditors to steal millions from the taxpayer."

Testified Kane, "An insurance company does not double and redouble its coverage of drivers it knows to be reckless." As for loans, "They are not available to openly insolvent firms from conventional sources."

"Shameful," says Kane when it comes to the government's implication that TBTF bailouts were good for the taxpayer. "On balance, the bail outs transferred wealth and economic opportunity from ordinary taxpayers to much higher-income stakeholders in TBTF firms. Ordinary citizens recognize this as unfair and officials that deny the unfairness undermine confidence in the integrity of economic policy making going forward."

As stated earlier, Kane has little use for the so-called reforms in Dodd-Frank and Basel III. Referring to the latter he points out the Basel Committee on Banking Supervision's 2013 "controlled frameworks." It is, he testifies, "build on fiction that all or most of the Systemically Important Financial Institutions or SIFIs can be persuaded to forego individually profitable credit business for the greater good." This is, he said, "awfully naïve."

So, if the taxpayer is being bamboozled by all this what's to be done? Kane calls on Congress to "declare that taxpayers have an equitable interest in any institution that can be shown to extract a subsidy from the safety net."

This would give the "taxpayer compensation for damages. A dividend in exchange for their implicit equity stake in the TBTF firm."

Next Kane articulated what I believe millions of Americans agree with. "Genuine reform," he said, "would compel the Department of Justice to prosecute megabank holding companies that engaged in easy-to-document securities fraud. As a legal person and convicted felon guilty BHCs (Bank Holding Companies) could be forced to break themselves up."

While he calls "living wills, an enhanced resolution authority and claw backs of undeserved executive compensation useful tools," he hammers hard at the practice of imposing fines saying it's "easy." Why? Because the shareholders pay them!

Kane further testified that in the current space it is very difficult for regulators to discipline individual managers of "influential and interconnected BHCs."

Kane asks the subcommittee to think of "Taxpayer equity in a TBTF as a trust fund and conceive of government officials as fiduciaries responsible for managing the fund."

In keeping with his taxpayer equity framework Kane testified "I find it disgraceful that corporate law legitimizes managerial efforts to exploit taxpayer's equity positions.

"The norm of maximizing stockholder value is inappropriate to TBTF firms. In TBTF institutions this norm leaves taxpayers an un-booked equity stake inferior to that of ordinary shareholders in five ways: 1) Taxpayers cannot trade their positions away, 2) Downside liability is not contractually limited, but upside gain is, 3) Taxpayer positions carry no procedural or disclosure safeguards, 4) Taxpayer positions are not recognized legally as an 'equitable interest,' and 5) TBTF managers can and do abuse taxpayers by blocking or delaying recovery and resolution."

Finally, as he concludes his testimony, Kane says, "If it were up to me, I would establish the equivalent of a military academy for financial regulators and train cadets from around the world. The curriculum would not be just to teach cadets how to calculate, aggregate and monitor the costs of the safety-net support in individual institutions and countries. The core of the curriculum would be to drill students in the duties they will owe the citizenry and to instruct them in how to confront and overcome the nasty political pressures that elite institutions exert when they become increasingly undercapitalized."

In closing he tells the committee, "Indiscriminately bailing out giant firms has hampered rather than promoted economic recovery."

As indicated, Dr. Kane expressed the need for prosecutions by the Department of Justice of crimes committed leading up to the GFC. In his book, "Predator Nation: Corporate Criminals, Political Corruption and the Hijacking of America," Charles H. Ferguson provides innumerable examples of prosecutable offenses.[2] Below is a sampling.

The chapter is titled "j'accuse." In it he supports the claim that among others, there was securities fraud, accounting fraud, perjury and RICO offenses.

He asks, "Where to begin?" because there is such a preponderance of evidence. For example, there are the violations of the Securities and Exchange Commission's Rule 10b-5. The rule states that "It shall be unlawful for any person, directly or indirectly, by use of any means or instrumentality of interstate commerce, or of the mails or of any facility of any national securities exchange to lie, cheat or steal."

Ferguson makes his case, "As we have already seen," he writes, "almost all the prospectuses and sales material on mortgage-backed bonds sold from 2005-2007 were a compound of falsehoods."

When discussing accounting fraud, he writes, examples abound! Among the most glaring were the inflated values proffered by major firms like Lehman, Merrill Lynch, and Citigroup when it came to the value of their property portfolios. Again, this is just one of myriad examples Ferguson dishes up.

Ferguson writes that in 1988 amendments were made to the federal mail fraud statute. Among them, "scheme or artifice to defraud includes a scheme or artifice to defraud another of intangible right to honest services." And in this regard, he holds the rating agencies accountable, stating, "With varying degrees of nakedness all three of the major rating agencies provided corrupt services to investors."

It is so discouraging that Kane's testimony and books like Ferguson's are not widely reported on. In essence the deafening silence they are greeted with leads us further into the abyss.

When reading Kane's testimony, I imagined it leading the nightly news with the anchor announcing, "Today on Capitol Hill, there was riveting testimony about the inherent unfairness of the financial system. So and so reports from Capitol Hill. And then a reporter would share the wisdom and analysis offered by Professor Edward J. Kane. Wouldn't that be nice?

Chapter Eight

BENEFIT SOCIETY?

"What if instead of bankers, we gave trillions of dollars to ordinary citizens running small businesses? Wouldn't that have saved us from a financial crisis, too? Or, what if instead we just let the little people earn a little interest on their savings accounts?"

---Al Lewis

It was February 2013 when William C. Dudley, the president and CEO of the Federal Reserve Bank of New York addressed the New York Bankers Association.[1] During his speech, he had this to say, "The issue of the social value created by market-based financial intermediation and appropriate scope and terms associated with the lender of last resort function are complex and ones that require further study." That said, he continued having kicked the can down the road. That can, being how does all this activity benefit society? In essence he said, we'll just put that off for another day.

In July of that same year Bruce Bartlett wrote an article in the *New York Times* titled, "Financialization as the cause of Economic Malaise."[2]

Referencing myriad research reports, he underscores the destructiveness of financialization. And, as you will see in this chapter, he is not alone.

Before I go on, I will share Investopedia's summation of the term "financialization." "Financialization is the increase in size and importance of a country's financial sector relative to its overall economy.

"The financial industry, with its emphasis on short-term profits, has played a major role in the decline of manufacturing in the U.S.

"A booming financial services industry has, however, led to growth in other sectors.

"In recent years, financialization has resulted in a massive increase in the amount and diversity of financial instruments being sold, a phenomenon known as securitization."

The most compelling quote in this article may be attributed to Adair Turner, Britain's former top financial regulator. According to Bartlett Turner said as follows, "There is no clear evidence that the growth in the scale and complexity of the financial system in the rich developed world over the last 20 to 30 years has increased growth or stability.

"Financial sector gains have been more in the form of economic rent—basically something for nothing—than the return to economic values."[3]

Circling back to income inequality Bartlett cites a report from the International Labor Organization, a United Nations agency, "financialization is by far the largest contributor (to income inequality) in developed economies."[4]

Breaking it down, the report estimates that 46% of labor's falling share resulted from financialization.

Two years later in 2015 renowned economist, Luigi Zingales, published a paper titled, "Does Finance Benefit Society?"[5]

Zingales could have shortened it considerably by answering his own question with the word, "no." But he did not. Instead, he equivocated. For example, he says a "positive role" by finance depends on how the public perceives it.

I would counter that statement with the observation that the public doesn't even know about it. It doesn't know about repo or collateral or securities lending et al.

A little over a year later economist and *Financial Times* writer, John Kay, delivered a speech at the Bank of International Settlements titled, "Finance is just another industry." Kay tells his audience, "Those who work in finance talk to each other, speak a language largely incomprehensible even to other businesspeople—and to an extent that defies the imagination—trade with each other." 6

And while Zingales writes that the finance industry has an "inflated" view of its benefits, just a few sentences down he writes, "...there is no theoretical or empirical evidence to support the notion that all the growth in the financial sector in the last forty years has been beneficial to society."7

You may recall that the trillions of dollars traded along those fiberoptic cables over our heads are largely trades in the secondary market—the wholesale funding market. Kay had this to say about that, "I have described the extraordinary value of secondary market trading that characterizes finance today. We are entitled to ask, 'What is it all for?' What are the economic and social purposes of this activity?"

He went on to say, "A country can only be prosperous if it has a well-functioning financial system but that does not imply that the larger the financial system a country has the more prosperous it is likely to be. It is possible to have too much of a good thing. Financial innovation was critical to the creation of an industrial society; it does not follow that every modern financial innovation contributes to economic growth. Many good ideas become bad ideas when pursued in excess."

Speaking of excess in the beginning of his speech Kay stated, "The total value of foreign exchange dealings exceeds the value of international trade in goods and services by a factor of almost one hundred. Total exposure under derivatives contracts is estimated by this institution (BIS) at $700 trillion—two to three times the value of all the assets in the world."[8]

I held onto Kay's speech for years. Literally, it was tucked into the side door of my car. I wrote atop it, "important." The reason was the directness of its content. Kay explained to his audience that "Finance can contribute to society and the economy in four principal ways." He said, "First, the payments system is the means by which we receive wages and salaries and buy the goods and services we need." Second, he said, "finance matches lenders with borrowers, helping to direct savings to their most effective uses. Third, finance enables us to manage our personal finances across lifetimes and between generations. Fourth, finance helps both individuals and businesses to manage the risks inevitably associated with everyday life and economic activity."

Kay accedes that most people in finance work in the areas of the first two principles, helping people with finance and seeing that payment structures are in place. Even the third principle is the purview of many finance employees.

He uses Barclays Bank as an example when he points out most bank employees make about $40,000 a year. These employees are concerned with the first three principles he lays out. The fourth principle, however, is markedly different with those working in that area earning anywhere from $500,000 a year to over a million dollars. And it is this principle, "risk management" that involves, you guessed it, wholesale funding. Kay says, "It is likely that 'the one percent' in Barclays Bank earn a total approaching half of the total wage and salary of this bank."

No doubt another reason I held on to this speech was Kay's recounting of a statement by Goldman Sach's CEO, Lloyd Blankfein. It would be funny were it not so serious. During a 2009 interview with the *Sunday Times*, Blankfein said his company was doing "God's work." Apparently, God had a hand in the firm's mission "to help companies to grow by helping them to raise capital. Companies that grow create cash. This, in turn, allows people to have jobs that create more growth and more wealth." He went so far as to call this a "virtuous cycle."

Kay dispels Blankfein's celestial posturing by sharing that helping business raise capital "was not, in fact, an important part of the business of Goldman Sachs. Raising capital for companies through underwriting and issuance of new debt and equity have accounted for less than 10% of the company's net revenues in the last five years." In fact, Goldman's profits, he said, "are mainly derived from secondary market trading in equities and the FICC."

Furthermore, Kay said, companies in general do not use firms like Goldman Sachs "to raise external capital." He added the practice, "has not been true for many years."[9]

Referencing a 2005 Jackson Hole symposium where Federal Reserve Chairman Alan Greenspan and Harvard president, Larry Summers were among the attendees, Kay, singled out another economist, Raghuram Rajan, who was also in attendance. And it just so happened was also there among BIS attendees. According to Kay, Rajan's 2005 prescience regarding the pitfalls of financial innovation was derided and dismissed by the Fed Chairman and his cohort with Summers going so far as to compare the prognostication to akin to choosing runners and horses over cars and airplanes. "Complexity," Summers argued, "was inseparable from progress."

Yet, what is created by financial innovation? Asks Kay. It is not like transport that "have brought us railways, cars, and planes. These innovations have transformed the daily lives of ordinary people. No one could say the same of forward exchange rates, credit default swaps or collateralized debt obligations.

"The risks swirling around Jackson Hole were those of share prices, exchange rates, and securities defaults. All of them are risks generated within the financial system itself."

As for the rest of us Kay is keen on what our concerns are. "Redundancy and unemployment...provision for old age...illness and mortality."

Like Bartlett, Zingales addresses the tremendous disparity when it comes to the acquisition of wealth when he writes that "The accumulation of great wealth by means which are not measured by the population at large, ...generate envy and resentment."9

The magnitude of riches is on display for all to see. Huge homes and lavish lifestyles. Whispers of Wall Street and its largesse circulate among the rest of us.

For whom among us know how a hedge fund works? It is not like the owner of a tractor company or a book publisher. These are professions we understand.

I have a friend whose cousin worked for a major bank. He got a $3 million bonus. She didn't know why, and that figure was permanently embedded in her brain. Often, she would bring it up. It bothered her that he, half her age, was able to acquire so much wealth and for what? I won't go so far as to say it rankled her, but it was clearly something she had trouble reconciling.

Adding insult to injury, Zingales writes that the finance industry is rife with fraud. According to him, "between 1996 and 2004 examination of (Dyck et al.) the cost of financial fraud among U.S. companies with more than $750 million in revenue is $380 billion a year."[8] He further states that the referenced study estimated that only a fourth of the fraud is detected. Thus, "...the annual figure can easily be four times the calculated amount!"[10]

Throughout the process of writing this book, I continue to peruse the internet for gems. Here's one I found on www.thefrontierpost.com.

Written by Mitchell Feierstein it is titled, "For 40 years I've watched 'rampant fraud' on Wall Street destroy capitalism, Covid-19 nailed its coffin."[11]

Harkening back to the crisis of 2008, Feierstein shares a quote from former Federal Reserve Chairman, Alan Greenspan. "I think there was rampant fraud in a lot of what was going on in these markets. We need to get far higher levels of enforcement of existing fraud statutes... things were being done that were certainly illegal and clearly criminal in certain cases, by which I mean fraud. Fraud is a fact. Fraud creates very considerable instability in competitive markets. If you cannot trust your counterparties, it won't work, and indeed, we saw that it didn't."

This malfeasance as we all know is coupled with the fact that once discovered, perpetrators are unpunished. Writes Zingales, "I am unaware of any financial executive going to jail for mortgage fraud or the LIBOR scandal." It appears Bernie Madoff stood alone as the financial perpetrator vilified in the press and sentenced to a life term, Zingales points out. It leads one to speculate had Bernie's business model been more sophisticated he too, may have got a pass.

Alluding to the business model that paved the way for the crisis, Zingales writes, "If the most profitable line of business is to dupe investors with complex financial products, competitive pressure will induce financial firms to innovate along that dimension with a double loss to society: talents are wasted in search for better duping opportunities and the mistrust towards the financial sector increases."

Regulatory capture and heavy lobbying contribute to what Zingales refers to as the "noncompetitive, plutocratic, clubbish" nature of finance. This is as opposed to the optimal "competitive, democratic and inclusive" type.

In an interesting aside, he shares that an academic who writes in support of solutions that would be "costly to banks" would be shunned by his peers, disinvited to conferences, etc.

Finally, he addresses the morality of those involved in questionable practices. One experiment cited (Cohen et.al) "...suggests that the business culture in the banking industry undermines honesty norm." This finding was further supported in another study (Wang et al.) which found "that the teaching of economics makes students more selfish and less concerned with the common good. Are we training people to be (more) dishonest?" he asks.[12]

The word cannibalism crept into my head when I read the following quote from Grant Williams' newsletter, "Things that make you go Hmmm..." [10] Williams is a well-respected British investor, advisor, writer, and interviewer.

In his July 2014 newsletter Williams wrote the following, "And now its warning lights are flashing red once again—about the disconnect between the buoyant financial markets and underlying economic realities, about a recovery which is too dependent on debt and unconventional monetary stimulus, about the depressing lack of productivity growth, about companies that prefer to downsize and buyback their own shares to investing in the future, about developing asset bubbles and the risk they pose to financial stability, and about the cowardly propensity of policymakers to take the easy option, rather than the tough decision to create a durable recovery."[13]

Yes, it was 2014 but the same could be said today.

I saved the best for last. The Kay quote that kept this article in my car for so many years. Because this quote is among the gems that sums up the problem succinctly. Here it is, "We need a finance sector to manage our payments, finance our housing stock, restore our infrastructure, fund our retirement, and support new business. But very little of the expertise that exists in the finance industry today relates to the facilitation of payments, the provision of housing, the management of large construction projects, the needs of the elderly or the nurturing of small businesses. The process of financial intermediation has become an *end in itself.*" [14] (my italics)

Chapter Nine

HEREIN LIES THE PROBLEM

"We can't eliminate Too Big To Fail...Because we have no resolve to do so."

--Thomas M. Hoenig

Admittedly, while I have read many books about finance and the crisis, I have not engaged with websites that purport to advocate for the so-called "little guy."

Among them is Better Markets. On its website it says in big letters, "Making the Banking System Work for All Americans and Not Just for a Select Few." On its testimonial page Massachusetts Senator Elizabeth Warren is quoted as follows, "Dennis Kelleher and his team at Better Markets have consistently pushed for financial reform that will help protect the U.S. economy from another financial crash. They are strong partners in the fight to level the playing field for middle-class families and have been persistent fighters for the American people, their jobs, savings, and retirements."

Kelleher is the founder of Better Markets. Former President Barack Obama is also on the page with the following quote, "Thank you, Better Markets." And others such as the late Senator Diane Feinstein echo Warren's praise. If it were true, we would be living in a different world today.

So, as Better Markets merrily strode along, I was oblivious. Perhaps, I should have engaged in it as part of my research for this book, but I didn't. Just knew about it, occasionally would drop by, and generally held it in high regard.

Periodically I would check out another similar site, WallStreetOnParade.com where recently, I discovered an invitation to "Grab an Easy Chair and Watch 21 Experts Explore the Path from the Collapse of Lehman Brothers to this Spring's Banking Crisis to the Urgency of Defanging the Mega Banks." The program was sponsored by Better Markets. I sat in my chair and watched the experts. It lasted seven hours.

Participants were the crème de la crème. The *New York Times* was represented as well as the *Financial Times*. Myriad authors of best-selling books about the crisis and its aftermath peppered the panels as well as lawyers, professors and none other than the Chairman of the Securities and Exchange Commission, Gary Gensler.

It was a star-studded event to mark the 15th anniversary of the fall of Lehman. Better

Markets claims it works for all Americans and not just a select few. You wouldn't know it by the likes of this effort.

From A to Z, it was a smorgasbord of everything that is wrong with the financial system. If one were to make a case for splintering it into a thousand pieces and scattering it to the wind, to borrow from President Kennedy, a stronger one could not be found than that made on Sept. 13, 2023, by Better Markets. Yet as you will see, exposing the financial system's considerable flaws does not pass the smell test when no solutions are to be found.

Here is a sampling of how the experts described the system that informs our lives. One said the system is "inefficient, dangerous and massively unfair." "A system designed for failure," said yet another. "I am horrified at what I saw and continue to see," said another going so far as to say the extent of intractability and politicization traumatized her. And the understatement of the day, "This is no way to run a railroad."

It was also telling when one participant skated near the very notion of creating a public alternative quietly stated that it is "politically extremely difficult to pass or even discuss at this point."

Not only were there no reformers on the panels but also missing were those who have produced irrefutable evidence that financialization has caused and continues to cause irreparable harm to the real economy, robbing the "all Americans," Better Markets claims to serve from an inclusive, democratic financial system.

At the conclusion of this seven-hour shitshow. I realized the problem was much, if it possibly could be worse than I thought. Why? Because the entire exercise consisted of hand wringing and a chorus of "I guess, we're stuck with it."

As far back as 2012, we had a path to true reform offered. "Restructuring the Financial System for Safety and Soundness," was co-written by Thomas Hoenig and Charles Morris. Mentioned earlier in this book, I said upon publication it was ignored. Not only by everyone else but also by its own author. Hoenig himself never advocated for his plan. Never insisted that the subject be raised in interviews.

Here is an excerpt from the paper, "The recommendation of this paper is to limit the safety net-and thus its subsidy-to what the safety net should protect by restricting banking organization activities by business line. Under the proposal, banking organizations would continue to provide the core services of commercial banks-making loans and taking deposits to provide payment and settlement, liquidity, and credit intermediation services. Other allowable services would be securities underwriting, merger and acquisition advice, trust, and wealth asset management." Furthermore, "Banking companies would not be allowed to conduct broker-dealer activities, make markets in derivatives or securities, trade securities or derivatives for either their own account or customers, or sponsor hedge or private equity funds." [1]

Hoenig was a participant at the Better Markets forum. At one point he brought up his 2012 paper which he said was ignored. Then he said, "We can't eliminate too big to fail...." Why? "Because we have no resolve to do so." Adding, "We are not willing to take the really disruptive action of simplifying the system, the structure and making it more functioning."

Think about what Franklin R. Edwards said in 1987 at Jackson Hole, "The idea that in some way the system may be seriously flawed is an alien thought. The notion that it should be drastically changed shocks us."[2]

And that is where we are today. Ironically the session he spoke at was titled, "Restructuring the Financial System."

Hoenig was among the first to put forth a blueprint for reform. Others have followed. Ellen Brown, Lev Menand, Morgan Ricks and Anat Admati are among them.

Brown's book "Banking on the People, Democratizing MONEY in the DIGITAL AGE," is a well-thought-out treatise offering common sense solutions aimed at ameliorating the wealth gap and restructuring the financial system.

More recently law professors, Lev Menand and Morgan Ricks, published a paper titled, ""Rebuilding Banking Law: Banks as Public Utilities." It too, was very impressive calling for a New National Banking system (NNB). As stated in the Introduction, "We believe that transitioning to the NNB system would be fairly simple—because virtually every feature of the system has a direct analogue or precedent in U.S. banking law." [3]

And there is Anat Admati and Martin Helliwig. Admati, a business professor at Stanford and Helliwig, a widely respected economist penned, "The Bankers' New Clothes: What's Wrong with Banking and What to Do about It-" in 2024. It's an update to a 2009 work by the same name. Its 350 plus pages with fine print regale the current system's flaws in excruciating detail combined with policy recommendations aimed at making the banks financially more stable.

Each of the works deserves the utmost respect and all are rooted in the ideal of creating an economic system that serves the greater good.

Yet none of their theses was articulated throughout the forum. Even Admati, failed to articulate recommendations made in her own recently published book!

And this silence transcends media and legislative efforts to reform the system. For all those trees felled in the forest to print these books and papers there is not a sound. No one hears. No one in a position of power does a darn thing!

And what better example of this than Better Markets or WallStreetonParade that promoted the forum. You won't find a story about the Menand/Ricks paper on their respective websites just as in 2012, Hoenig's paper was never even mentioned in the press. They pretend to be part of the solution when in fact they are part of the problem.

So, you can see why I became angry watching the Better Markets dog and pony show. Especially because it was titled "Can TOO BIG TO FAIL Be Ended, and, if so, how?" Weird how "if so, how?" is in small letters. Even in their banner they betray themselves as being cowed by the system.

The hypocrisy of Better Markets and others like it is stunning. I guess you could say if true reform were realized there would no longer be a market for Better Markets, or all the authors on the panels who reap the financial rewards of writing about market dysfunction.

And while papers like Menand and Ricks' hold apparent promise there is something else afoot. That is the idea, that those at the epicenter of the shadow banking system have devised a plan of their own. A plan that has been decades in the making, codified in law. A plan that renders all reformers—moot.

Read on.

Chapter Ten

THE DOOMSDAY MACHINE

"You'll own nothing. And you'll be happy."

---2016 World Economic Forum Video

Forty years ago, I worked for an AM radio station as a news anchor/reporter. There was an engineer named Walter.

It turns out, he read an earlier version of this book and reached out. It was nice to hear from him after so many years. He sent me a link to www.thegreattaking.com. And this changed everything. I felt very fortunate to have had Walter send this to me. Why? Because as shocking as the book, "The Great Taking" is, I know enough to know it is all true.

"The Great Taking" is written by David Rogers Webb. Years ago, as a computer savvy young man Webb secured himself a job on Wall Street as a technician. This enabled him to work with a wide array of Wall Street players, giving him a unique perspective. It exposed him to the backdoor operations of his clients. They included investment banks, commercial banks, brokerage houses, bond houses and even the DTC. He was baptized by fire.

He went on to work in mergers and acquisitions and run a very successful hedge fund.

Fast forward to decades later. He is a farmer living in Sweden. And this is the locale from which he wrote "The Great Taking."

A subsequent search by this author has revealed that everything he writes about has been hiding in plain sight. Buried in legal papers unbeknownst to practically everyone else in finance. Only those who wrote these substantial works that often exceed 100 pages, knew of what Webb would awaken the world to in "The Great Taking." And what did these papers draw from? The Uniform Commercial Code.

I plead guilty to the oversight in my own research for this book. When writing about safe harbor I focused solely on the fact that it exempted repo and other securities transactions from the automatic stay in bankruptcy. What I failed to find out was not only were the transactions exempt, but that the financial institutions, custodians et al. via provisions in U.C.C. had senior creditor standing. This means in the event of an institutional failure that collateral consisting of securities purchased by investors is not returned to them in kind. It means that the financial institutions themselves take ownership and the rest of us get what's left over. If anything.

The subject of Webb's book is mainly Article 8 of the U.C.C. code. The revisions he addresses took place in 1994 and were promulgated by the American Law Institute and the National Conference of Commissioners on Uniform State Laws.

Among the architects of Article 8 is attorney James Steven Rogers. In a 1996 paper he discloses how obscure these adjustments are in the wider world. One can only surmise this was done accidentally on purpose. "Article 8 is one of the more recondite branches of commercial law. Neither the generalist practicing lawyer, nor the commercial expert is likely to feel comfortable with this subject."[1] He goes on to say it is not commonly taught in law school. You get the point.

Thirty years later the true nature of these "revisions" are laid bare and beginning to reverberate. Webb tells an astonishing tale in its implications. In a world where derivative trading has reached astronomical proportions with up to a reported $2 quadrillion awash in the global economy.

Webb begins his book with the following, "If you prefer, consider this a work of fiction or perhaps the ravings of a madman."[2] He fully expects his readers to be incredulous because the book is about "...the taking of collateral, all of it, the end game of this globally synchronous debt accumulation super-cycle. This is being executed by long-planned, intelligent design, the audacity and scope of which is difficult for the mind to encompass."[3]

You, no doubt, have seen the picture put out by the World Economic Forum showing a smiling young man with the caption "You will own nothing. And you'll be happy."

According to Webb, that is exactly the plan, and he has the goods to back it up.

Put another way, Webb states, "There are now no property rights to securities held in book-entry form in any jurisdiction."[4]

As someone who worked in finance, I looked back on the days of stock certificates with nostalgia. The idea of having a document in hand showing your part ownership of a company had a certain magic to it, a point of pride.

What laid the groundwork for where we are today was the conversion in the 1960s and

70s of holdings to book-entry whereby stocks were traded in "street name." "Street name" meant the brokerage held the security "on behalf of" the investor. Electronic trading was born. All the while the investor was understood to be the rightful owner. To this very day, we all believe this to be the case.

Webb dispels this with his revelation that unbeknownst to us the U.C.C. altered the very structure of stock holdings and ownership with its designation of "Security Entitlement."

He writes, "Ownership of securities as property has been replaced with a new legal concept of a 'security entitlement,' which is a contractual claim assuring a very weak position if the account provider becomes insolvent."[5] That is, "...instead of owning shares, investors are only eligible for a pro-rata share of residual assets. This includes investors who have prohibited use of their funds as collateral."[6]

At the time of Rogers' writing half of the 50 states had adopted the Article 8 changes. Today all of them are on board. It was stealth, hidden away from even the most sophisticated investment professionals.

All of this wouldn't work were it relegated simply to the U.S. so of course, in

2004 the European Commission Internal Markets and Services Director General played a role in the creation of The Legal Certainty Group. This group, Webb tells us, supersedes all others in its global reach. Its creation had one aim to ensure, "collateral can be taken immediately and without judicial review by entities described in court documents as 'the protected class.'"[7]

In his book, he shares documentation of these directives. He also addresses clearing and settlement issues, noting that should a large clearing platform fail, there too, assets have been legally attached to the senior creditor class. That is, the financial institutions themselves. All bases have been covered.

Furthermore, it's Webb's contention that the CCPs in Europe and the U.S. are designed to fail. Only to be replaced by new CCPs owned and operated by the secured creditors.[8]

And what of the bailouts? There won't be any says Webb, "It has been promised that there will be no taxpayer bailout this time—as if that is a good thing. Why? Simply because this will allow the banks to be closed rather than nationalized. Then all deposits and assets will be taken by the 'protected class' of secured creditors. This is where this is going."[9]

Earlier in this book, I wrote that the repo market was fueled by debt. And this is the catalyst for the proliferation of transactions of all shapes and sizes. Debt is at the root of the entire shadow banking system and says Webb, "The bottom line is that debt has for centuries had the function of dispossessing, of taking away property, capital and investments from someone else."[10]

In hindsight the views of Luigi Zingales and John Kay seem "quaint" considering the enormity of what Webb has to say. Small wonder they and their ilk are kept under wraps. It speaks to the futility of articulated decency and morality when up against a tsunami of nefarious, duplicitous and evil intent.

I encourage you to read Webb's book. His thesis has been vetted by the most respected financial analysts and to a person, no one has disputed its veracity.

The book is free online at www.thegreattaking.com.

As of this writing two states have presented bills to remove the most egregious language from Article 8. That is, to restore ownership of assets to the investors. Neither has succeeded but by their very introduction these bills have raised awareness of the situation.

I will end with a couple of quotes from Webb. First, "To not know is bad. To not want to know is worse." [11] And second, "This needs to be unwound legally and peacefully...We need lawyers. It's about giving people their 'stuff' back and not hurting people."[12]

Chapter Eleven

IN THE NAME OF RISK

"Legal rules that do not insulate
intermediaries from adverse claim liability are
rules that create systemic risk."

--Professor James Steven Rogers

In the wake of The Great Taking, I
decided to look back and see exactly what was
being written about Article 8 in the Uniform
Commercial Code at the time of its revision in
1994.
That was the time when there was a
quiet, intrepid, calculated circumvention
undertaken by the National Conference of
Commissioners on Uniform State Laws and
the American Law Institute that open the
floodgates to untraceable trading activity that
has in the subsequent decades grown to
unfathomable levels
As mentioned in the previous chapter, in
essence the "entitlement" ends the property
rights of the individual investors. Boston
College law professor, James Steven Rogers,
again previously mentioned, played a large
role in the Article 8 revisions and in his 1996

paper, "Policy Perspectives on a Revised Article 8", he wrote, "The term 'security entitlement' can then be used as a convenient shorthand for 'the package of rights that a person who holds a securities position through an intermediary has against that intermediary and the property held by that intermediary'."[1].

If one were to question the rationale of what's to follow, it is, according to Rogers, the control of systemic risk. And what better way to address that than through mastering the clearing and settlement process. Wrote Rogers, "...the provisions of Article 8 that warranted the most careful attention were those commercial law rules that have a direct bearing on the objectives of clearance and settlement reform."[2] Who better to quote than the man himself, Alan Greenspan, "...my experience with financial crises has convinced me that the greatest threat to the liquidity of our financial markets is the potential for disturbance to the clearance and settlement process for financial transactions. "[3]

What I found online regarding the 1994 changes were legal papers. Some in favor, some opposed. All were rife with incredibly dense language and for the most part, exceeded 100 pages in length. Primarily I focused on the points raised by Webb.

Two terms ubiquitous in the literature are "indirect holding system" and "fungible bulk."

In short, the "indirect holding system" is a system without any correlation between investors and their securities. "Fungible bulk" is made up of all the securities. Merriam Webster describes fungible as follows, "being something (such as money or a commodity) of such a nature that one part or quantity may be replaced by another equal part or quantity in paying a debt or settling an account." And Cede & Co.* is in most instances the shareholder of record. Rogers affirms this, "If one examined the shareholder records of large corporations whose shares are publicly traded on the exchanges or in the over-the-counter market, one would find that one entity-Cede & Co.* is listed as the shareholder of record of somewhere in the range of sixty to eighty per cent of the outstanding shares of all publicly traded companies."[4] And this was in 1996.

One of the first items I came across in my travels was a sleight of hand on the part of the revisionists. This was accomplished by

*Nominee name for The Depository Trust Company, a large clearing house that holds shares in its name for banks, brokers and institutions in order to expedite the sale and transfer of stock.

placing the burden of proof of malfeasance on the investor all the while knowing that as Rogers himself put it, it is "...*logically impossible* to assign any nonarbitrary answer to the question 'who was first' even if we had complete and accurate records."[5] (my italics) Driving the point home is Florida State University law professor Larry T. Garvin who wrote in a1999 paper titled, "The Changed (and Changing?) Uniform Commercial Code" that "Most fundamentally, Revised Article 8 expressly abandons all tracing rules."[6]

The upshot is our securities disappear into the maw of the intermediary and transferee accounts with no oversight, no tracking, nothing. Ergo, according to Rogers, "The commercial law of securities transfer has been based on the notion that it is *affirmatively undesirable* for counterparty or others involved in implementing securities transfers to bear the burden of investigating the propriety of persons known to be acting for others."[7](my italics) If they do not bear the burden who does?

Rogers writes essentially that investors are laden with the risk that comes when no one is minding the store. "Realistically, there simply is not anything that commercial law rules can do to eliminate or minimize this risk.

Nothing that one says in commercial law rules is going to change the very simple proposition that if someone steals your property, it will not be there anymore. Regrettably, the alchemists were wrong; gold cannot be produced out of nothingness."[8]

He goes on to say, "One cannot decide whether a given rule is good or bad for investors by asking whether it imposes liability on intermediaries or exonerates intermediaries."[9] In other words, intermediaries are viewed as amoral entities, not to be messed with.

And what of those on the other side of the trades? The transferees. Under the revised Article 8 investors whose holdings have, unbeknownst to them, been transferred to another financial firm are powerless to regain them due to the fact the receiving entity acted in "good faith."[10] Rogers puts it this way, "Saying that 'owners' can get 'their property back' if an intermediary wrongfully transferred it just means that some other 'owners' are going to get their 'property' taken away."[11] So, as the Gershwin brothers would say, "Let's Call the Whole Thing Off."

And a big surprise, the revisions are designed to ensure that the repo market is unimpeded. In his paper Garvin writes, "In addition, a rule which protected entitlement holders over secured creditors or, for that matter, transferees, would greatly complicate repo financing, for it is far from clear even now whether repos are true sales or security interests."[12]

Rogers does not leave us without examining the FDIC and SIPC. Yes, they are there to protect investors but as evidenced by recent bank failures, they fall woefully short. What does Rogers think about that? "Though an awareness of the existence and operation of the regulatory and insurance systems is an important element in a realistic assessment of the risks that investors face in holding through intermediaries, one's assessment of the adequacy of these systems is essentially *irrelevant* for purposes of understanding and assessing Revised Article 8."[13](my italics)

At least two papers critical of the revision of Article 8 pointed out that it was formulated by lawyers who counted among their clients' major banks and brokerages. The SEC and the Fed also had a role in its creation. That it was carried largely outside of the purview of the general investing public was not a surprise to St. John's University law professor Francis J. Facciolo who wrote in his 1997 paper, "Father Knows Best: Revised

Article 8 and the Individual Investor", that "Faced with such recondite and complex issues, what consumer representative will invest the hundreds, if not thousands of hours necessary to understanding these disparate but not thousands of hours necessary to understanding these disparate but related areas of law?"[14]

Answering his own question Facciolo wrote, "Funding is needed for consumer representatives to participate in the revision process. These consumer representatives must participate from the very beginning, rather than being invited to comment at a later point in the drafting process."[15]

To say all of this was done "on the quiet," would be a vast understatement. In a 2001 paper "Indirectly Held Securities and Intermediary Risk", Duke University business professor, Steven L. Schwarcz observes, "It is theoretically possible for the Rule to be implemented as a treaty, but such a formal approach appears unnecessary and might raise unwarranted political hurdles."[16]Ya think?

Professor Facciolo perhaps said it best back in 1997, *"The triumph of the financial institutions is complete* and not even the few crumbs offered by the Article 8 Bar Report are left for investors."[17] (my italics)

NOTES

Introduction

1. Mary Ellen Tuthill, *Rated Money Fund Report*, Feb. 7, 2007

2. Daniel Covitz, Nellie Lang, Gustavo A. Suarez, "Evolutions of the Financial Crises-Panic in the Asset-Backed Commercial Paper Market," Federal Reserve 2009

3. William C. Dudley, "Restoring Confidence in Reference Rates," Oct. 2, 2014

4. Lev Menand, Joshua Younger. "Money & the Public Debt: Treasury Market Liquidity as a Legal Phenomenon," pg. 233

5. Lev Menand, Joshua Younger, ib. Cit pg. 234

6. Professor Saule Omarova of Cornell University – "The U.S. Comptroller of the Currency Nominee and Her Writings: What They Mean for Banks & Fintech," published by Gibson, Dunn & Crutcher LLC, Sept. 27, 2021

7. Franklin R. Edwards- "Can Regulatory Reform Prevent Impending Disaster in Financial Markets?" Federal Reserve of Kansas City Jackson Hole, Wyoming symposium "Restructuring the Financial System" – August 1987

8.	Ellen Brown, "Banking on the People, Democratizing MONEY in the DIGITAL AGE," Pg. 358

9.	Mary Fricker from her presentation "Shadow Banking in Plain English"- presented at the 11th Annual Conference and Society Conference-Advancing Business Journalism and Convergence- University of South Carolina School of Journalism & Mass Communication- Sept. 27-28, 2012 (available on YouTube)

10. Janet Yellen, Financial Crisis Inquiry Commission testimony

11. Thomas M. Hoenig, president of the Federal Reserve of Kansas City, Charles V. Morris vice-president, "Restructuring the Banking System to Improve Safety & Soundness, "May 2011

12. William C. Dudley, "Fixing Wholesale Funding to Build a More Stable Financial System," Feb. 2013

13. E. Gerald Corrigan, Fed president of New York, "Overview" at 1987 Jackson Hole Symposium, "Restructuring the Financial System."

14. Professor Saule Omarova-Comments in Gibson, Dunn & Crutcher release on her nomination to the post of Comptroller of the Currency- Sept. 27, 2021

15. Investopedia

16. Mary Fricker, ob. Cit

17. Garyl B. Gorton "The Panic of 2007"
Gary B. Gorton
National Bureau of Economic Research
September 2008

18. William Dudley, ob. Cit

19. Sarah Butcher, efinancialcareers.com on
Zoltan Pozsar-July 2021

20. Zoltan Pozsar, Tobias Adrian, Adam
Ashcraft "Shadow Banking" 2010- Federal
Reserve Bank of New York

21. Danielle DiMartino, "Fed Up," Pg. 123

Chapter One: Repo

1. Josh Galper, "We Size Repo Market at $13.4
Trillion," Aug. 3, 2021

2. Jeffrey Chang & David Wessel, "What is the
Repo Market? And why does it matter"
Brooking Institute, June 28, 2020,

3. Tobias Adrian, Brian Begalle, Adam Copeland
& Antoine Martin-"Repo and Securities Lending"
Federal Reserve Bank of New York -2013

4. TradingEconomics.com/overnight repo rate

5. Mother Jones, Kevin Drum, 2010

6. Sara Foster, "The repo market, explained — and why the Fed has pumped hundreds of billions into it" Bankrate Sept. 10, 2021

7. Jennifer Taub "Time to Reduce Repo Risk" by Jennifer Taub, The New York Times, April 4, 2014

8. Michael Quint, "Lessons in Drysdale's Default" -The New York Times-May 10, 1982

9. "Money & the Public Debt," by Lev Menand and Joshua Younger, pg.

10. ibid. pg.

11. Michael Quint, "Big 5 U.S. Securities Dealers" -The New York Times-June 9, 1983

12. Scott Skrym, "Two Bankruptcies That Created the Modern Repo Markets," www.scottskrym.com April 3, 2013

13. "Money and the Public Debt," by Lev Menand and Joshua Younger, pg.

14. www.infoplease.com , 1980 money-market fund rates

15. Scott Skrym, "Two Bankruptcies That Created the Modern Repo Markets," www.scottskrym.com April 3, 2013

16. The Financial Crisis Inquiry Report, January 2011, pg. 31

17. Thomas H. Hoenig, president and CEO of Federal Reserve Bank of Kansas City and Charles S. Morris, vice-president of Kansas City Fed "Restructuring the Banking System to Improve Safety and Soundness"

18." Tobias Adrian, Brian Begalle, Adam Copeland and Antoine Martin-"Repo and Securities Lending Federal Reserve Bank of New York 2013

19. Securities Industry and Financial Markets Association website (www.simfa.org) "U.S. Repo Market Fact Sheet"

20. International Capital Markets Association online mission statement (www.icmagroup.org)

21. (pg. 45) Office of Financial Research website, "Legal Entity Identifier" (www.financialresearch.gov)

22. Bank for International Settlements "Simple, transparent and comparable securitization" – "Criteria for identifying STCs" July 5, 2017

23. International Capital Markets Association June 21, 2017, Repo Video (www.icmagroup.org)

24. Securities Finance Times, June 2021

25. Christopher Leonard, "The Lords of Easy Money," pg. 244

26. Darrell Duffie, "Financial Regulatory Reform After the Crisis: An Assessment," pg. 40

Chapter Two: The Drysdale Affair

1 James Rowe, Jr. & Merrill Brown, "Through Abrupt Personality Change Tiny Wall Street Firm Demonstrates the Allure and Danger of Speculation" - the Washington Post -May 23, 1982

2. Ron Scherer "How Drysdale Affair Almost Stymied US Securities Market"- The Christian Science Monitor- May 27, 1982

3. www.workers.org, "Financial Ruin at Drysdale and Penn Square," July 20, 1982

4. Michael Quint, "Lessons in Drysdale's Default"- The New York Times- May 20, 1982

5. Robert J. Cole "Chase Bank Will Pay Off Interest Owed by Defaulting Bond Dealer" - – May 20, 1982

6. Randall Forsyth "Anyone Remember the Collapse of Drysdale?" — May 18, 2011

7. "Two Bankruptcies that Created the Modern Repo Market"- Scott Skyrm- www.scottskrym.com

8. Michael Quint, "Lessons in Drysdale Default," The New York Times, Jan. 31, 1983

9. www.workers.org-

10. Michael Quint, "Lessons in Drysdale Default," The New York Times 1983

11. www.workers.org, Alfred Gaylord Hart's Letter to the Editor of The New York Times – May 31, 1982

12. United Press International- July 27, 1983

Chapter Three: Lombard Wall & Safe Harbor

1.Robert J. Cole "Wall Street Firm Files for Bankruptcy" The New York Times- August 13, 1982

2. Carolyn Sissoko, "The legal foundation of financial collapse" University of West England-published by the Social Sciences Research Network-Oct. 6, 2009

3. Nathan Garalnik "Bankruptcy -Proof Finance and the Supply of Liquidity"– Yale Law Journal Vol. 122, pg. 460

4. Jeanne L. Schroeder, "Repo Redo: Repurchase Agreements after the Real Estate Bubble"- Professor at Yeshiva University's Benjamin N. Cardozo School of Law-March 16, 2012- published by the Social Science Research Network

5. Gary Walters, "Repurchase Agreements and the Bankruptcy Code-Need for Legislative Action"- - Fordham Law Review-Vol. 52, Issue 5, 1984

6. Jeanne Schroeder- "Repo Madness: The Characterization of Repurchase Agreements under the Bankruptcy Code and the U.C.C. (Universal Commercial Code)- Jeanne Schroeder-(cited above) 1996

7. ibid. pg.56

8. Carolyn Sissoko, "The legal foundation of financial collapse," pg. 6

9. ibid. pg. 10

10. ibid. pg. 9

11. Carloyn Sissoko, "The legal foundation of financial collapse." pg. 11

12. Ibid, pg. 15

13. ibid. pg. 13

14. ibid. pg. 16

15. ibid. pg.17

16. Edward R. Morrison, Evans Gerber Professor of Law at Columbia Law School & Mark J. Roe, a David Berg Professor of Corporate Law, Harvard Law School & Christopher S. Sontchi, United States Bankruptcy Judge District of Delaware, "Rolling Back the Repo Safe Harbors" pg.1016-1071

17.Paul L. Lee, Banking Law Journal
18. Edward R. Morrison, Evans Gerber Professor of Law at Columbia Law School & Mark J. Roe, a David Berg Professor of Corporate Law, Harvard Law School & Christopher S. Sontchi, United States Bankruptcy Judge District of Delaware, "Rolling Back the Repo Safe Harbors" pg.1017

19. ibid. pg. 1017

20. David Rogers Webb, "The Great Taking," pg. 30

21. ibid. pg. xxviii

22. Scott Skrym, "Two Bankruptcies That Created the Modern Repo Markets," www.scottskrym.com April 3, 2013

Chapter Four: Collateral

1. Sebastian Infante, Charles Press and Jacob Strauss "The Ins and Outs of Collateral Re-use" by
(University of Minnesota) -Dec. 21, 2018 - Federal Reserve Bank of New York

2. Mary Fricker from her presentation "Shadow Banking in Plain English"- presented at the 11th Annual Conference and Society Conference-Advancing Business Journalism and Convergence- University of South Carolina School of Journalism & Mass Communication- Sept. 27-28, 2012 (available on YouTube)

.3. Sungard's April 15, 2005, paper: "Collateral Optimization: The Next Generation"

4. Depository Trust & Clearing Corporation website: www.dtcc.com

5. Mark Whitney, "Repo, Baby, Repo" - www.counterpunch.org – 10-23-13

6. Jeffrey Snider-Alhambria -Contra Corner- 2014

7, Richard Comotto- "A supplementary note on the systemic importance of collateral and the role of the repo market" Senior Visiting Fellow ICMA Centre, Henley Business School, University of Reading

8. Adam Kirk, James McAndrews, Parinitha Sastry
and Phillip Weed- "Mixing and Matching Collateral
in Dealer Banks" April 1, 2014-Federal Reserve
Bank of New York

9. www.efinancemanagement.com regarding Reg
T & Rule 15-c3-3

10. Adam Kirk, James McAndrews, Parinitha
Sastry and Phillip Weed- "Mixing and Matching
Collateral in Dealer Banks" April 1, 2014-
Federal Reserve Bank of New York

11. James Brunsden, John Glover, Bloomberg, -
-European Commission Report excerpt August
2013

11. Sissoko, ibid.

Chapter Five: Repo's Cousin

1. Mary Fricker from her presentation "Shadow Banking
in Plain English"- presented at the 11th Annual
Conference and Society Conference-Advancing Business
Journalism and Convergence- University of South
Carolina School of Journalism & Mass Communication-
Sept. 27-28, 2012 (available on YouTube)

2. Tobias Adrian, Brian Begalle, Adam Copeland, Antoine Martin, "Repo and Securities Lending "Feb. 2013

3. Mary Schapiro-Securities and Exchange Commission Roundtable on Securities Lending- Sept. 29, 2009

4. Tobias Adrian, Brian Begalle, Adam Copeland, Antoine Martin "Repo and Securities Lending -Feb. 2013

5. Securities Finance Trust Company "Securities Lending Best Practices" published by the 2015

6. "Deutsche Funds Securities Lending Overview" -Deutsche Bank

7. Financial Stability Board "Policy Recommendations to Address Structural Vulnerabilities from Asset Management Activities," 2017

8. Deutschebank website: March 31, 2022

9. Americans for Financial Reform Education Fund submission to the SEC re: proposed Rule 10c-1, April 1, 2022

10. Securities Finance Trust Company, ibid.

11. DataLend website- www.datalend.com

12. Interos website- www.interos.ai

13. S&P website-www.standardandpoors.com

14. Reuters – "I regret any harm:' Short seller compensates target in rare move" June 22, 2021

15 Katia Porzecanski, Tom Schoenberg, and Matt Robinson- "Hedge Funds Face Expansive Short-Selling Probe, Exciting Critics," Bloomberg Dec.10, 2021

16 Josh Galper, ", "Intraday Securities Lending Data and a Securities Lending Ticker." Finadium, April 2012

17. Gary Gensler, "SEC Proposes Rule to Provide Transparency in the Securities Lending Market" Nov. 18, 2021

18. SEC Proposes Short Sale Disclosure Rule, Order Marking Requirement, and CAT Amendments, Feb. 15, 2022

19. Financial Stability Oversight Council Annual Report, 2020

20. R. Smith, Anthony Pijertov and J. Justin Paget "Sailing Without Headwind: Structured Lending Market Embraces Bankruptcy Safe Harbor Provisions" -- Hunton Andrews Kurth law firm.

Chapter Six: Current Issues

1. Frank M. Keane, "Securities Loans, Collateralized by Cash: Reinvestment Risk, Run Risk, and Systemic Risk" - "Current Issues" – Federal Reserve Bank of New York- Nov. 2013

Chapter Seven: Taking Stock

1, Boston College Finance Professor, Edward J. Kane "Statements on Measuring the Funding Advantages Enjoyed by Large, Complex and Politically Powerful Bank Holding Companies"- Testimony before the Finance before the Financial Institutions and Consumer Protection subcommittee of the U.S. Senate Committee on Banking and Urban Affairs

1. Charles H. Ferguson "Predator Nation: Corporate Criminals, Political Corruption and the Hijacking of America" by Charles H. Ferguson- Chapter "j'accuse"

Chapter Eight: Benefit Society?

1. William C. Dudley, President and Chief Executive Officer – "Fixing Wholesale Funding to Build a More Stable Financial System" Remarks at the New York Bankers Association's 2013 Annual Meeting & Economic Forum, February 1, 2013

2. Bruce Bartlett, "Financialization as the cause of Economic Malaise" - The New York Times July 2013

3. Adair Turner – former chair of the UK's Financial Services Authority

4. International Labor Organization – United Nations on financialization and income inequality

5. Luigi Zingales, "Does Finance Benefit Society?" 2015

6. John Kay, "Finance is just another industry" - speech before the Bank for International Settlements -May 2016

7. Luigi Zingales- "Does Finance Benefit Society?" 2015

8. John Kay, "Finance is just another industry" - speech before the Bank for International Settlements -May 2016

9. Luigi Zingales- "Does Finance Benefit Society?" 2015

10. Mitchell Feierstein "40 years I've watched 'rampant fraud' on Wall Street destroying capitalism, Covid-19 nailed its coffin"- - www.frontierpost.com – March 21, 2020

11. Luigi Zingales- "Does Finance Benefit Society?" 2015

12. Grant Williams "Things that make you go Hmmm...2014

Chapter Nine: Herein Lies the Problem

Better Market Commentors:
--Simon Johnson, Professor of Economics & Management, MIT
--Gary D. Cohn, writer
--Anat Amati, Professor of Finance & Management, Stanford University
--Arthur Wilmarth, Professor of Law, George Washington University
--Saule Omarova, Professor of Law, Cornell University

1.Thomas M. Hoenig and Charles Morris, "Restructuring the Financial System for Safety and Soundness," pg.1
pg. 159

2. Franklin R. Edwards, "Can Regulatory Reform Prevent Impending Disaster in the Financial

Markets?" Federal Reserve Jackson Hole
Conference, August 1987

3. Lev Menand and Morgan Ricks "A Ten-Point
System for Making Banking a Public Utility,"
pg. 1

Chapter Ten: The Doomsday Machine

1. James Steven Rogers, "Policy Perspectives on
Revised U.C.C. Article 8" June 1996

2. David Rogers Webb, "The Great Taking" pg. vii
3. Ibid., pg. 1

4. Ibid., pg. 7

5. Ibid., pg. 10

6. Ibid, pg. 10

7. Ibid., pg 10

8. Ibid, pg. 29

9. Ibid., pg. 49

10. Ibid., pg. 61

11. Ibid, pg. 63

11. Interview on "The Daniela Carbone Show,"
YouTube, Jan. 2024

Chapter Eleven: In the Name of Risk

1. James Steven Rogers, "Policy Perspectives on Revised U.C.C. Article 8" June 1996, pg. 1451

2. Ibid., pg. 1461

3. Ibid., pg.1438

4.Ibid., pg. 1443

5.Ibid. pg. 1516

6. Larry T. Garvin, "The Changed (and Changing?) Uniform Commercial Code", pg. 323

7. James Steven Rogers, "Policy Perspectives on Revised U.C.C. Article 8" June 1996, pg. 1553

8. Ibid., pg.1520

9. Ibid., pg. 1497

10 Ibid, pg. 1521

11. Ibid., pg. 1523

12. Larry T. Garvin, "The Changed (and Changing?) Uniform Commercial Code", pg. 334

13. 1. James Steven Rogers, "Policy Perspectives on Revised U.C.C. Article 8" June 1996, pg. 1539

14. Francis J. Facciolo, "Father Knows Best: Revised Article 8 and the Individual Investor", pg. 620

15. Ibid., pg. 620

16. Steven L. Schwarcz, "Indirectly Held Securities & Intermediary Risk", pg. 296

17. Francis J. Facciolo, "Father Knows Best: Revised Article 8 and the Individual Investor", pg. 660

Recommended Reading

www.repowatch.org Repowatch.org is the site launched by award-winning financial journalist, Mary Fricker. It is the go-to place for all things repo and shadow banking.

"Banking on the People: Democratizing MONEY in the DIGITAL AGE" by Ellen Brown

"The Creature from Jekyll Island: A Second Look at the Federal Reserve" by G. Edward Griffin

"Rebuilding Banking Law: Banks as Public Utilities."
  https://www.vanderbilt.edu/vanderbilt-policy-accelerator/banks-as-public-utilities/

"Restructuring the Banking System for Safety & Soundness" by Thomas M. Hoenig and Charles Morris
  https://www.fdic.gov/about/learn/board/restructuring-the-banking-system-05-24-11.pdf

"The Great Taking by David Rogers Webb
www.thegreattaking.com

"The Bankers' New Clothes-What's Wrong with the Banking System and What to Do About It" by Anat Admati & Martin Hellwig

NOTES: